9 LIVES
OF A FIGHTER PILOT

One pilot's personal story as an American patriot

by
Colonel Gregory G. Raths, USMC (RET)

A Lightning Source Book
Published by Lightning Source
1246 Heil Quaker Blvd., La Vergne, TN USA 37086

© Copyright 2013 by Gregory Raths
Book design by Dori Beeler
Cover design by Dori Beeler
Edited by Sandra Rea, Master Marketing & PR

For information regarding special discounts for bulk purchases,
please contact Lightning Source at: inquiry@lightningsource.com
Phone: (615) 213-5815

ISBN: 978-0-615-74049-2

Every effort has been made to make this book as complete and as accurate
as possible. However, there may be mistakes, both typographical and
in content.

*The purpose of this book is to educate and entertain. The stories are based on real-life events.
Names may have been changed to protect identities and privacy. The author and publisher
shall have neither liability nor responsibility to any person or entity with respect to any loss
or damage caused, or alleged to have been caused, directly or indirectly, by the information
contained in the book.*

**If you do not wish to be bound by the above, you may return
this book to the publisher for full refund.**

9 LIVES
OF A FIGHTER PILOT

*One pilot's personal story as an
American patriot*

by
Colonel Gregory G. Raths, USMC (RET)

DEDICATION

Dedicated to my father
John A. Raths
and to the memory of my mother
Viola C. Raths
and her sister
Rita M. Jorgensen

ACKNOWLEDGEMENTS

First, I thank my parents and siblings. My mother kept me on the straight and narrow during my developing years. My father was my inspiration to become a military pilot.

Second, I give special thanks to my oldest brother Bob who supported me throughout my life. He was always there when I needed guidance or help.

Third, to my wife Luci I give tremendous thanks. She kept our family together during my many long stretches of military deployments. Her love and devotion kept our family intact as a single loving unit. I will always remember all you have done for me. I love you.

Finally, I thank my military mentors: Fighter Squadron Commanding Officers Major General Tim Ghormley, Colonel Jim French and Colonel Ron Richards. These were my seniors who helped to shape me as a leader. I looked up to them for guidance and wanted to be a leader like them. I hope I have made them proud!

TABLE OF CONTENTS

·— X —·

FORWARD

I've had a fantastic life. I want you to have the same. If you have dreams and aspire to be the best in your chosen profession, I want you to know you can absolutely achieve your goals. While one reason I wrote this book is to leave a written account of my life as a legacy for my children, so they will know who I am years from now when no one is around to tell the grandkids about me, another reason is really simple. I want young people to know that if I could achieve my goals to become a military fighter pilot and then to work at the White House for our Commander-in-Chief, then they can reach their goals, too. I'm dead serious about this. All it takes is a plan and a little fortitude. Luck helps, of course, but luck as they say is where preparation meets opportunity.

Don't get me wrong. This is not to say that I don't believe in luck. I do. I've been really fortunate in my life not just because I recognized and grabbed hold of opportunities, but because I didn't lose my life several times when I could have. That's why I titled this book as I did. The way I see it, I sort of used up eight of my "lives" already. I'd better make the best of this ninth!

As you read through these pages of my life (or lives), you will see that it could be said that Death stalked the parameters of my activities as a jet pilot just hoping for his opportunity to hit me in the head with his scythe. That's being a bit dramatic, but looking back I can see just how lucky I was not to lose my life when the arresting hook on my jet hit the back of an aircraft carrier or when I blacked out pulling too many Gs one afternoon in my early career as a pilot. Or how about that time my aircraft caught fire, or my jet actually exploded on the ground, or I hit a flock of birds immediately after takeoff?

These are lucky near misses. But these events come with the territory when you're a Marine jet aviator. And near misses are more common than you might think in war. For example, in Desert Storm I was darned close to being hit by three Iraqi surface-to-air missiles! Another time a scud missile hit our base. No near miss that time, but I'm still here.

Then there are those times in everyday life where I can count my lucky stars. Like my recent motorcycle accident. I could have been far more injured than I was. As a retired pilot I still have a need for speed, you might say. The wild hair still exists and can get a man in trouble from time to time, like when he's on his motorcycle. All it takes is a slick patch, a little poorly placed gravel or another driver who doesn't see you and it's goodbye, Dare Devil. Or in my case, goodbye, man who knows the dangers of the road and had an accident already. Either way, I walked away and I feel mighty fortunate.

In this book you are going to read of a man's life, his goals, how he reached them, what he did with opportunities he saw, and how important the support of family and friends can be to the outcome of his life. That man is me. This is my story…

SECTION ONE

EARLY LIFE: THE FORMATIVE YEARS

Every story has a beginning. Mine is a humble one. There was no trauma and no incidents of horror in my childhood that will make you cringe. Rather my path was laid out early in life. I may not have known I'd be a fighter pilot one day, but there are few things I never doubted. I was loved, and my parents had my back at every turn. Nothing beats support when it comes to raising one's children! I want to begin with my formative years and how I grew up in a large family in Arizona.

CHAPTER 1

It was late at night and I lay awake in my bed, eyes wide open. I was worried about aliens invading my hometown and, worse yet, invading my bedroom. As a young child I had just watched a horror film with my brothers on our family's black-and-white television. I pretended it didn't bother me, but in the movie humans would fall through soft sand along a dusty road near a farmhouse, and then the Martians would take them captive and stick a long needle in the back of their necks. I did not want one of those creatures sticking anything in my neck!

I looked over at my brothers' beds. We shared a room in our small Phoenix home where there was barely enough room to fit two bunks. They were all soundly asleep. I slept on the bottom bunk. I looked up at the underside of my brother Steve's bunk above. The sound of his breathing from that top bunk was sort of comforting, but I didn't think it had the power to keep aliens at bay. I could see directly across to my oldest brother, Bob, who was asleep on the top bunk of the other bed. I could see my brother, Ron, just a year older than me, out like a light on the bottom bunk across the room. I was four years old at that moment in time. The year was 1957. My sisters, Jean and Mary Ann, were sleeping in their bedroom across the hall. My youngest siblings, Theresa and Dan, hadn't been born yet, and my parents were down for the night in their bedroom at the end of the hall.

I tried to fall asleep as thoughts of the invading Martians raced through my head. Finally, I gave into temptation to run out of my room. But wait, I knew I would have to move less quickly. I wouldn't want to call attention to myself if any aliens happened to be monitoring us.

I slowly got out of bed, sure that the Martians would grab me at any moment. They didn't. I must have had a protective bubble, because I made it safely to my parents' room at the end of the hallway. Maybe it was my colorful cowboy-print pajamas that saved me as I hustled down the dark, narrow hall past the clothes hampers. I walked to my mother's side of the bed and shook her shoulder. She woke and looked at me with unfocused eyes. I clearly had raised her from a deep and peaceful slumber.

"What's wrong, Sweetheart?" she asked. She put her arms out to me.

"I'm scared from the movie we watched before we went to bed. What if the Martians come for me?"

My mother smiled and told me to wake my father. I could lie next to him. Relieved, I did as she requested. My dad could keep me safe! This is one of my earliest memories of how protected my parents always made me feel. Every child should feel so safe.

When I reached my dad's side of what seemed to be the largest bed I've ever encountered, I shook his shoulder and told him I was scared. A man of few words, he moved toward the middle of the bed and said, "Get in, Son."

I snuggled next to my dad, feeling his warmth and strength. Now I could sleep. A couple of hours later, or maybe it was just moments after I'd fallen asleep, I could feel the muscles of my dad's arms as he picked me up and carried me down the hallway to my bedroom to put me back into my bed. As he laid me down on the mattress, I felt the coolness of my sheets and the softness of my pillow as it welcomed my head back into place. I was no longer scared of anything as I quickly went back to sleep and finished the night in the comfort of my own bed. Just knowing my dad was down the hall was enough for me at that moment.

CHAPTER 2

My parents moved to Phoenix from the cold, icy grip of
Minneapolis in 1952, their four young children – Jean, Bob,
Steve, and Ron – in tow. Times were simpler then. Mom and
Dad hitched a trailer to their Plymouth and headed west. My
father found a job at the local Phoenix newspaper. Arizona
would be the place my folks would make their home and their
future ... and a few more children.

Just a few months later, at St. Joseph's Hospital on September
12, 1953, I was born. The first Raths' child to be born in the
west! My sister Mary Ann was born three years later, Theresa
five years after that, and then my youngest brother Dan in
1965. I always wondered what people must have thought
seeing my mother in town with her eight children. However,
it was a different time and large families were not uncommon.
My best friend growing up, Nick Ganem, had six brothers and
sisters; a high school girl friend, Kathy McMahon, had ten
children in her family; and our neighbor had nine. The Baby
Boomer generation was flourishing in Phoenix. But why were
we from Minneapolis?

My father, John Allyn Raths, was born in Minneapolis in 1918,
and grew up in Minnesota and Wisconsin. He attended De La

Salle Catholic High School in Minneapolis and graduated in 1936 in the midst of the Great Depression. Understand that this was a time in our history when not a great many young adults completed school. A lot of them had to drop out to help put food on the table. My father attended school and helped feed his family.

After high school he continued to live with his parents in a small house on North Aldrich Avenue in central Minneapolis with his younger brother, Albert. My dad's father worked as a farm equipment salesman with his territory, covering eastern Minnesota and western Wisconsin. After my father graduated from high school he found a job at a local print shop, and later with war imminent in Europe, he joined the military. That was in 1941, and he would become a radioman. My dad entered the military to be a pilot, but he needed two years of college. So that was that. Hearing him tell this story planted a seed for me. Maybe I could be a pilot one day. It sounded pretty cool.

My mother, Viola Clara (Schwartz) Raths, was born in 1919 and grew up in East St. Louis, Illinois, on a horseradish farm. Her father worked his entire life on that farm. They called it a "truck farm" back then, because the farmers would load their crops on a truck and take them to market to sell. East St. Louis, just across the Mississippi River from St. Louis, Missouri, was a rural area with hundreds of truck farms scattered across thousands of acres. Life was hard, but everyone pitched in to help one another. They didn't know that life was hard. It was simply life.

My mother's mother was a homemaker who died giving birth to my Aunt Rita in 1933. My mom, just 13 at the time of her mother's death, was crushed with the passing of her beloved mother; she would carry a heavy heart the rest of her life. True to the times in which she lived, my mother was suddenly forced to step into her mother's shoes to be the woman of the house and help raise her sister. Some young women in her day in similar situations would have quit school, but mother persevered, graduating high school in 1937. However, she didn't go on to attend college. She stayed home to do the cooking and cleaning for her father and older brother. His name is Evarist who let me ride along on his tractor a few times.

Though it seems like a harsh decision now, young Rita was placed in St. John's Catholic Orphanage nearby to be reared and taught by the Catholic nuns. In that time children were placed in orphanages to give them a chance at an easier life. That was the theory anyway. My mom and her father visited Rita often. Sunday was visiting day, and Rita anxiously awaited their visit each and every week. Many of the orphans would be adopted and leave the orphanage, but that could only happen if the child's parents, if they had parents, allowed the adoption. Rita's father gave strict orders that Rita could never be adopted. Considering the difficult living circumstances, mom and Rita wrote letters to each other often and became very close.

A friendly neighbor, Mrs. Bass, who lived near the farm asked to take care of Rita, but her father would not approve of that either. The man's heart was hard; he was tough as nails and made my mother work very hard around the farmhouse while he was out tending the crops. By all accounts, my mother's life was difficult. She eventually left home, and when Rita turned 14, her father had a replacement for my mother around the home. It was then that Rita was returned to the farm to take on the housework and cooking. Goodbye, Viola Clara; hello, Rita! It was as if the women in my grandfather's life were interchangeable, but again it was a different time and things were tough all over.

When my mother was 21, she helped out at a nearby military base, Scott Field, in Belleville, Illinois, handing out coffee and donuts to the troops after Sunday Catholic Mass. There she met my father who was going through radioman school and preparing for combat in Europe. After several weeks of small talk with my mother on Sundays, my dad finally got the nerve to ask her out on a date. That was in November 1941. They agreed to meet at the town square in Belleville. Romance blossomed. They chose a date to see each other again … December 7, 1941. This turned out to be a rather fateful day in history, and their date would be postponed. That was the day the Japanese attacked Pearl Harbor. All military personnel were restricted to base and Scott Field was closed to all civilians. Their dream date had to wait awhile, but eventually my parents got together to continue their romance. My grandfather was not pleased that my mother had a boyfriend. My mother had other ideas. So did my father. They would continue seeing each other, no matter what. Not too long after, they would be wed.

In 1942, the military waived the college requirement for flight training, so my dad took the required exams and physical, and was cleared for flight school. He would be a pilot after all. This was a proud moment for him. He was transferred to Mississippi for flight training, and my mother moved near the base to be close to him. Goodbye, farm life. On May 27, 1943, my parents were married at the chapel at Columbus Field in Mississippi. They needed to move quickly before my dad was shipped off to Europe and the war.

With World War II raging, my father finished flight training at Will Rogers Field in Oklahoma City and was sent to Europe in March 1944 to begin combat missions with the 644th Squadron of the 410th Bombardment Group assigned to the Ninth Air Force in England. My dad flew the twin-engine Douglas A-20 Havoc attack bomber. His squadron helped prepare for the invasion of Normandy with multiple bombing missions along the French coastal defenses, on German airfields in France and railroad yards in Belgium. My dad participated in the D-Day invasion by flying two combat missions on June 6, 1944, bombing gun positions and railway choke points along the Normandy coast. He told me stories about that day. As he approached the coast of Normandy he was amazed at the thousands and thousands of ships and landing crafts off the coast. The day prior he recalls there were none, and now thousands. "Where did they all come from," he thought. He told me, "This was truly a surprise attack on the Germans."

Later that summer, he would assist ground forces at Caen and St. Lo, France, in July 1944, and at Brest, France, in August and September 1944 by bombing bridges and railroad lines. As a boy, I couldn't get enough of these little tidbits of my father's life as a participant in the war! His Bombardment Group moved to France in September 1944, and through mid-December 1944 they continued to fly combat missions against German railroad bridges, marshaling yards and communications centers in support of the Allied assault against the German Siegfried Line. He then participated in the Battle of the Bulge from December 1944 to January 1945, flying multiple bombing missions against German railheads and bridges. This offensive was a last-ditch attempt by the Germans to reverse the course of the war. It cost the lives of many without producing any lasting success. My father was awarded the Bronze Star, Distinguished Flying Cross and several Air Medals for his heroic achievement in aerial flight during the war. After 65 combat missions he received orders to return to the states.

Growing up, I loved hearing all of his war stories and his tales of being an attack bomber pilot. He told me that on one mission over Germany, he was shot up so badly from anti-aircraft gunfire, that the cable leading from the flight controls to the rear elevator had only two strands remaining on the cable. Those two frayed strands kept his crew and him alive.

One day when I was a kid he took out his medals that he'd buried in a drawer in his bedroom dresser and showed them to me. All I could say was, "Wow." I didn't know it then, but with his stories, the seed that had been planted was sprouting! One day I'd follow in my father's footsteps. I would be a military pilot.

While my father fought battles abroad, my mother was fighting them on home turf. Pregnant with her first child, she refused to go back to the farm to live with her father. Instead she would live with my father's parents in Minneapolis. My eldest sister, Jeannette, entered the world on July 13, 1944. My father wouldn't see her until he returned from the war in 1945.

CHAPTER 3

Aunt Rita moved to Phoenix two years after my parents did
to start a new life of her own. She was just 20. She had enough
of the farm life with her father and brother. She found a nice
little apartment near our house. My parents originally rented
a small house in West Phoenix, but when I turned one year old
they bought a house where I was raised until I left home at age
18. To help with the mortgage payments my parents rented a
room out for a year. Our home was the former rectory for the
priests of St. Gregory's Catholic Parish. The priests lived in the
house waiting for their permanent rectory to be constructed
on the parish grounds. Once the priests moved into their
new residence, we moved into our home, which happened to
be right across the street from St. Gregory's Catholic School
and Church, where I would attend elementary school and
be taught by nuns. There was rarely a chance for me to miss
school. It was literally steps away from my front door.

The year 1954 marked the reunion of my mother and her sister,
but that's not all. In December of that year, just two months
after my first birthday, it marked a frightening life event for
me. One day I awoke very sick and could hardly breathe.
I developed double pneumonia as a result of an allergy. I
was rushed to the hospital and given a slim chance to live.

In fact, one night my doctor stayed with me till morning to see how I responded to the medication. He was almost certain I wouldn't make it. I slept in an oxygen tent and after several days I was breathing much easier. I spent Christmas in the hospital. Through prayer, western medicine, personal attention and grit I came through with flying colors to return home just before New Year's Day. My family truly had something to celebrate at the dawn of 1955!

Maybe my brush with death gave me a little extra grit that year, because I became determined in all that I did and didn't want to do. For example, when Aunt Rita found a husband a few years after she came to Phoenix, she wanted me to be her ring bearer. The happy couple was to be married at St. Gregory's Church on Thanksgiving Day, 1958. My response to the ring bearer request? "No, no, no!" At five years of age, I wasn't thrilled with the idea of walking up the long aisle in a crowded church. They'd have to bribe me first. And so they did.

For the reasonable terms of just one crisp dollar bill I agreed to carry Aunt Rita and Uncle Bob's rings while wearing a classy white tuxedo and grinning from ear to ear. Brother Bob was the altar boy for the ceremony, and once I got to the altar, he took the rings from the pillow I carried in my small, entrepreneurial hands. My job was over. An easy buck. Cha-ching! I was still smiling as I walked to a pew to sit down. Aunt Rita and Uncle Bob were like second parents to me. I saw them quite often. They didn't live far from us. They chose the neighboring town of Glendale to call their home. I loved them dearly. They would have three children, my cousins with whom I would grow up and grow closer to over the years.

I began first grade at St. Gregory's in 1959. I was the fifth Raths child to attend, so the nuns knew the name well. My mother was in the Women's Club, and my father a member of the Men's Club as well as Scout Master of the Church's Boy Scout Troop 43. With my parents so involved in the church I couldn't just blend in with the other 45 students. We all sat quietly in the large classroom with our hands folded on the desk when our teacher, Sister Damian, walked into the room.

Sister Damian was a force to behold. Tall and imposing in her long, black tunic with a white coif and black veil, she could look a bit frightening. Her ensemble was completed by a large rosary around her waist with the crucifix that hung down the front of her tunic. As her students, everyone in the class stood up in unison when Sister Damian entered the room. We then recited a short prayer and then turned to the American flag on the sidewall to pledge allegiance to the United States with our right hands over our hearts. When Sister Damian took roll for the first time in our class and came to my name, she said, "Well, hello, young Gregory. Welcome to the first grade."

"Oh, no," I thought. She already knows who I am. I'd have to watch myself. I didn't want her reporting any bad deeds to my parents. My formal education now en route, Sister Damian (a name that gives great irony now) taught my class the alphabet, addition and subtraction, and also art and music. I did okay and was on the path to a great education. But education wasn't all that was on my mind.

CHAPTER 4

At the age of six I took my first job. With the aide of my trusty little red wagon I delivered milk to the nuns at the St. Gregory's Convent. First, I had to pick up the empty glass bottles from the convent, then walk to the neighborhood milk store (Rovey's) and bring the full bottles back to the convent's back door. Looking back, this is a unique story. I didn't know then that I was doing something that not very many little boys could do. I received a whole nickel on each trip that I brought home and put into my piggy bank. Having endured the Great Depression, my mother was a stickler for savings. She taught me well. After earning a few more nickels, she took my brother Ron and me to the Arizona Bank just down the street from our house and opened saving accounts for us. She then took us to the Social Security Office, where we received our Social Security cards. I learned the value of a dollar and the value of saving. I thank my mother. (As for the use of my Social Security number, I would learn the point of that later in life!)

My father worked at the Phoenix Gazette and Arizona Republic newspapers in downtown Phoenix as a typesetter. At first he earned $3.25 an hour, and he worked hard for that small pay. He walked four miles to work so my mother could have the car during the day. A member of the typographical union, my dad became the leader of the local hall. He didn't make enough money to feed all the kids, pay the mortgage and pay for private school tuition. That meant he had to take a second job. On weekends my father mowed lawns around the neighborhood. He brought his sons – Steve, Ron and me – with him to help out with the lawn work. We got to know our neighbors well. We worked from dawn till dusk mowing lawns, trimming hedges and raking leaves. The old push mower we used was so heavy that Ron and I had to get on each side of the thing to push it through the thick Bermuda grass. I remember how the grass catcher would quickly fill up. We would later get a power mower that made mowing much easier.

At the end of a long day of mowing lawns, especially in the hot Arizona summer sun, we were all sore and exhausted. We'd pile into our 1956 Ford station wagon with all the lawn gear in the back. Before we headed home, my dad always stopped by the local bar, the Yo Yo Tavern on Indian School Road. His three young boys sat at a table where we'd be treated to a Coca Cola. We sat and chatted while we watched our dad at the bar with his friends. He always drank a couple of ice-cold draft beers and ate a pickled sausage. It's funny how I can remember the little things; it's the mundane details that make up our lives.

At the tavern my eyes roamed to the scantily clothed women on the posters and calendar on the walls. My dad would look back to us from the bar and say, "Eyes on the table, boys," adding his gentle smile. Dad usually gave us a dime to play the electronic bowling game while he was at the bar. Taking turns to shuffle a puck down the wooden lane to hit certain spots that would lift the plastic pins, we laughed and were thankful to be a part of our dad's day.

At home we each received our share of the profits: 50 cents to each boy; my dad took the rest to pay bills. The next business day, we were off to the Arizona Bank to make a deposit. I loved watching my savings account grow. Back then fifty pennies could go pretty far. Plus, there was a sense of pride among my brothers and me about being part of taking care of the family. It may have bonded us closer than had we not helped dad with the weekend mowing jobs, but we weren't the only ones pulling our weight. Mom did a lot, too.

CHAPTER 5

A stay-at-home mom, my mother had her hands full with us kids, but found time to be a Cub Scout leader and Brownie leader. She also watched several children after school to pick up a few extra dollars to help put food on our table. A devout Roman Catholic, my mother took us to Catholic Mass every week. On Sunday evenings, we would go to Benediction and pray the rosary at St. Gregory's Church. My mother made sure that we meditated at each Station of the Cross during Lent. She was strict about our religion, and she was strict at home.

We had a daily routine. After school, we kids were allowed to watch one hour of television. Looking back, it's funny to think we only had a handful of channels to watch. When I explain this to youth, they look at me with a glazed expression. Channel 5 had a lot of my favorite shows, like the Wallace and Ladmo Show, which was full of cartoons and silly skits. My mom fed us cookies and Kool-Aid. Once the show was over, it was time for homework. No debating allowed.

While we kids studied, my mother prepared the evening meal, usually a variation of macaroni and cheese, canned ravioli or spaghetti; rarely did we have meat for dinner. On occasion we would have fried chicken, and even more rarely we had steak that was barbequed on the outside grill. That was a treat! My dad would grill one large steak and cut it up for all of us. For dessert, it was normally canned peaches or fruit cocktail. I remember fighting with my brothers over the two half cherries in the can of fruit cocktail. Also, milk was on the menu every night; we were told it was good for our bones.

After dinner my brother Ron and I washed the dishes. It was our assigned chore. We alternated weeks on who would wash and who would dry. Once the dishes were done my mom would take us kids on a walk with Mary Ann or Theresa in the stroller. We usually walked about a mile to a horse pasture where we would pull up grass and feed the horses. On the way home we stopped at Dairy Crème, where we each got a five-cent vanilla ice cream cone. A cone dipped in chocolate was seven cents, but we didn't have the extra pennies for that special treat. Once we got home it was back to our homework.

My mother had a very smooth system when it came to running her house. My dad would usually take a nap after work, or work around the house taking care of the big jobs, such as painting or working on the car. My mom would sit with us individually once our homework was done to see if we had finished everything the nuns had sent home with us. Once our homework was complete we each had to read for at least an hour.

Every Saturday my mother took us to the Phoenix Library on Central Avenue to check out books to read for the week. These things, while they seem rather boring or routine, were helping to set the stage for a certain order I'd take into my life as an adult. Without order there is chaos; with chaos we accomplish nothing. Perhaps if my family hadn't had its rules I wouldn't have become a pilot, I wouldn't have worked at the White House for the Commander-in-Chief and I wouldn't have gone on to lead a productive life. This passes my mind a lot.

There was no room for complaining as I grew up, because my mom had no mercy if we misbehaved, but she wasn't cruel. Punishment varied from writing 100 to 300 times, "I must be obedient to my mother at all times," or getting a swat on the rear end with her famous red wooden stick that she kept on the shelf in the laundry room. The worse punishment was when she would say, "Wait until your father comes home," which no kid wants to hear. In hindsight I have to laugh, because the "big" punishment from my father wasn't all that big of a deal. It was one good swat on the behind with his big hand. The fear that came before his arrival home was the real punishment. Pure torment!

My parents were good at saving money. They each had their ways, For example, once a month after dinner, Dad would cut our hair in the back breakfast room. One by one we boys took the chair and got our buzz cut. Later in life, when I went into Marine Corps training, the buzz cut by the military barbers took just about the same amount of time... 30 seconds. The military barber was the first professional barber I ever received a haircut from in my life.

Mom knew how to save money, too, and she always made it seem like a lot of fun. On occasion, when our home needed a piece of furniture, mom would pack some of us kids in the station wagon and we would go to the furniture auction. Mom would look around at the used furnishings in the large showroom and when she saw a piece she wanted she would bid on that piece. It was so much fun for us kids to watch the auctioneer rattle off his jargon, pointing to different people, and ending things by saying, "SOLD! To the lady with the four kids!!" After the auction, mom would complete the paperwork, and within a couple of days, the furniture would be delivered. I actually thought for years that this was the way people bought furniture. Little did I realize that there were actual furniture stores with new furniture!

At home in the evenings each of us kids would parade through the shower in the back bathroom to get cleaned up and ready for bed. This was followed up with brushing our teeth, getting into our pajamas and kneeling on the side of our bed to say our night prayers. Once we were all in bed, my mother would come to each of our beds and kiss us goodnight and cover us up, and reassure us that our Guardian Angel would watch over us throughout the night. I said a little extra prayer to keep the Martians away.

See? I told you that it was a pretty good childhood; one I wish that every child in the world could have. I've done my best to replicate the parenting I received with my own children. We'll get to that later.

To say, however, that my childhood was idyllic is a little off. Even we had our missteps growing up.

CHAPTER 6

When I was in grade school, my oldest sister, Jean, attended Xavier Catholic High School for girls in Phoenix and my older brothers, Bob and Steve, went off to the Franciscan Seminary in Santa Barbara, California for high school. My dad took on a third job as a janitor to help pay for the increasing cost of our education. My parents even took in a foreign exchange student from Guatemala, Blanca Gutiérrez, who lived with us for a year. She was the same age as Jean and they went to school together where they became the best of friends. They remain so even today.

With two of my brothers away at school, my father's parents moved in with us during the winter months to get out of frozen Minneapolis. Our house became a game of musical beds when Bob and Steve were home from the seminary for the Christmas holidays. If all the beds were full, we pitched a tent in the backyard. One or more of the kids would get to sleep there for a while. We didn't mind. It was like a backyard adventure, and Arizona winters are mild.

When my sister graduated from Xavier she went off to Mundelein College in Chicago and joined the BVM convent. My mother was on Cloud Nine. My sister was studying to become a nun, and two of my brothers were in the seminary to become Franciscan priests. My mother's prayers were being answered. As a member of the St. Anthony Guild in Phoenix, she was required to have a child in religious studies. She qualified. My mother may have had intentions of me following in my brothers' footsteps, but I was a little different.

It was in my fourth-grade year when the differences were becoming more apparent. That's when I was given the nickname "swivel neck" by my teacher, Sister Sylvester, since I tended to look around at other students' papers during tests. After a parent-teacher conference my mother was quick to rid me of that nickname. She made me write the following more than 100 times, "I must not look at other students' papers."

At home I was becoming the "problem child." As the fifth of eight kids I tried to stay under the radar, but that wasn't working out for me. I enjoyed teasing my little sisters, which usually ended up with them telling mom on me. I also enjoyed harassing our neighbor's dog, Wags. Our neighbor had no problem letting my parents know of my shenanigans.

My mother often threatened to send me to the Fort Apache Indian Reservation in Northern Arizona to live with the Indians if I didn't behave. Obviously, this was merely a threat, but it did help straighten me out. I had no desire to live with the Indians. In my mind it would have been like the old west days. It also made me daydream about what it would be like to live in a teepee. That might have been interesting.

CHAPTER 7

Every year I looked forward to spring, because my dad would take us boys to Major League Baseball spring training games. Several teams came to the Phoenix area to train. I followed the San Francisco Giants and was a big fan of Willie Mays, the Giants' all-star center-fielder. One spring training game, we arrived late to Casa Grande Stadium. As we were walking from the parking lot to the stadium, a foul ball flew into the parking lot that I grabbed for a souvenir. A few minutes later another foul ball flew toward us and landed in the exact same spot, so I grabbed it, too. Before I even got into the stadium I had two baseballs! For a young boy in that day, and maybe even today, that was a real thrill. I enjoyed walking into the stadium and seeing the beautifully manicured baseball field with the crisp white chalk lines going down each foul line. The white square bases and the perfectly groomed pitcher's mound were works of art in my mind. Once I got to my seat and settled in, I asked a fan who hit the two foul balls into the parking lot. The offender was none other than Willie Mays! I cherished those balls and kept them in my bedroom for years.

In typical fan fashion, I bought a transistor radio with an earpiece, and at night I would listen to the Giants' games in my bed. I kept a scorecard and penciled in the hits and runs for each batter. I loved it when the Giants' Hall of Fame broadcaster, Russ Hodges, described a home run: "It is hit deep to left field, is it? Is it? Yes it's a bye-bye baby."

Russ Hodges was famous for his legendary call in the 1951 final playoff game when the Giants played the Dodgers for the pennant. The Giants won the first game, the Dodgers the second, with the Giants taking the tie-breaking third game with a dramatic ninth-inning home run by Bobby Thomson, a play known as the "Shot Heard Round the World." I will never forget reading his words in an old baseball magazine. (This proves how big a fan I am, I guess.)

Said Hodges, "Bobby Thomson... up there swingin'... He's hit two out of three, a single and a double, and Billy Cox is playing him right on the third-base line... One out, last of the ninth... Branca pitches... Bobby Thomson takes a strike called on the inside corner... Bobby hitting at .292... He's had a single and a double and he drove in the Giants' first run with a long fly to center... Brooklyn leads it 4-2...Hartung down the line at third not taking any chances... Lockman with not too big of a lead at second, but he'll be runnin' like the wind if Thomson hits one... Branca throws... There's a long drive... it's gonna be, I believe... THE GIANTS WIN THE PENNANT!! THE GIANTS WIN THE PENNANT! THE GIANTS WIN THE PENNANT! THE GIANTS WIN THE PENNANT! Bobby Thomson hits into the lower deck of the left-field stands! The Giants win the pennant and they're goin' crazy, they're goin' crazy! HEEEY-OH!!! I don't believe it! I don't believe it! I do not believe it! Bobby Thomson... hit a line drive... into the lower deck... of the left-field stands... and this place is goin' crazy! The Giants! Horace Stoneham has got a winner! The Giants won it... by a score of 5 to 4... and they're pickin' Bobby Thomson up... and carryin' him off the field!"

I waited for the time the Giants would win a pennant in my lifetime and in 1962, when I was nine years old, the Giants won the National League pennant with 103 wins. I was so excited to listen to the World Series on my radio. The games were all played during the day, so I brought my radio to school and listened to the play by play during recess and lunch hour, sometimes slipping the earpiece in during class without the teacher's knowledge. Unfortunately, the Giants lost to the New York Yankees in seven games. Game Seven was at Candlestick Park in San Francisco, and the Giants lost 1 to 0 in a real heartbreaker of a ball game. Baseball had now become my passion, but that's not all. I was also an avid Boy Scout.

CHAPTER 8

In fourth grade I joined the Cub Scouts and began a five-year period of scouting, which culminated with my Boy Scout Eagle Award just after graduation from the eighth grade. My three older brothers had all earned their Eagle Scout Award, and my mom would not let me be her first son without the award. My mom was my den leader in Cub Scouts, and my dad was my scoutmaster in Boy Scouts, which made scouting great fun for me. I have a lot of fond memories of my scouting years!

Even before I went into scouting my dad loved to take us boys on long hikes throughout central Arizona when he had some free time. He once took us hiking deep into the Superstition Mountains just east of Phoenix to the famous Weaver's Needle and Lost Dutchman's Mine, but our most memorable and challenging hike was down the Grand Canyon when I was nine. We all hiked down the canyon along the steep Kiabab Trail, spent two days camping on the bottom of the canyon next to the Colorado River, and then hiked back up the more gradual Bright Angel Trail. What an accomplishment! What a memory. The canyon was so beautiful with the chiseled rock formations and the beauty of the various colored canyon walls. The mighty Colorado River snaked its way through the gorges, cutting the canyon deeper into the earth. Throughout the hike we stopped often to rest, but also to take in the beauty of such a magnificent canyon.

My Boy Scout troop met every Wednesday night at St. Gregory's social hall. It was in these meetings that I would learn a lot of things that would help prepare me for life. Of course, I didn't know it at the time! For example, one weekend a month our troop camped out in the wilderness at different locations throughout central Arizona and we learned how to live off the land. That would come in handy later in my military training.

Every summer I attended a weeklong scouting session at Camp Geronimo, alongside the Mogollon Rim in Northern Arizona between Payson and Pine. Camp Geronimo was managed by the Theodore Roosevelt Boy Scout Council that was headquartered in Phoenix. A number of Scout troops shared the camp each week and all the troops participated in scouting events, including hiking, fishing, archery, swimming, first aid and other outdoor activities. I had a great time at camp with my friends from school. We all learned a great deal during our summers. It was during one of these camps when I was 13 that I got my first taste of leadership... and I liked it. I became a Boy Scout patrol leader. So did my friend, Nick.

Nick and I were tight. In the summer we went on scouting trips together; in the fall Nick's dad took us dove hunting. It was deer hunting in the winter. I never shot a deer, but I was able to hit a few doves with a 12-gauge shotgun. Looking back, it's pretty amazing, that I bought that gun at such a young age! (Times have changed.) I knew the power of that weapon and I respected it. When Nick and I joined the National Rifle Association (NRA), we took a course on gun safety. Only then would our parents allow us to begin hunting.

CHAPTER 9

In the summers I didn't just camp and do the scouting
adventure thing, I also worked mowing lawns, delivering
flyers for the local super market and going door to door to sell
everything from Christmas cards to light bulbs. When I turned
11, I landed an afternoon paper route, delivering 57 papers
along my neighborhood route. For all my hard work and time
spent delivering the Phoenix Gazette I earned about $6 a week.
These jobs helped me become a businessman at a young age,
which meant I never had to ask my parents for money. If I
wanted a new baseball glove, I saved up to buy one, and if I
wanted a new bicycle, I'd buy one when I had the money in
my pocket to do so. That taught me to be independent and
self-reliant. I've tried to pass these qualities to my children. So
far, so good!

Every summer I was kept really busy. When I wasn't working,
hanging out with Nick, hunting, fishing and scouting, I took
swim lessons. Every morning I'd show up at the neighborhood
swimming pool, Nelson's pool, run by Elwood and Rosemary
Hunt. The pool was only a mile from my house. By today's
standards that might seem far, but it was a quick bike ride for
me with friends. Looking back, it seems like a scene out of
The Andy Griffith Show, we'd pay our 25 cents each morning

to take our swim lesson. For the most part, we did it not only to learn to swim but rather to hang out with each other for a couple of hours. Life was simple then. I look back at that time in life with gratitude. It was a time when kids could be kids.

In the evenings I played baseball at a nearby public school, Clarendon Elementary, which sponsored little league baseball. From age six to 13, I played every summer in one baseball league or another. I remember putting my baseball glove on the handlebars of my bike and pedaling to the school for baseball practice or games. The competition was tough, but it helped to prepare me for high school sports. My brother, Bob, coached me one year and found our team a corporate sponsor with the unfortunate name of Mary Gay Eggs. While other teams were named for a sporting goods store, a lumberyard or a bicycle shop, we were the Gay Eggs. Needless to say we got some real ribbing from the other teams when we ran onto the field with Mary Gay Eggs on our uniforms. The picture brings a smile to my face even now. Thanks, Bob!

CHAPTER 10

All through grade school I made friends easily. Academically I had trouble with writing and reading comprehension, but I thrived in mathematics. When I was in the seventh grade, modern algebra was being introduced and I really enjoyed working on the math problems. In the eighth grade I won a trophy for mathematics. Man, was I proud!

My pal Nick and I were an inseparable duo. We were always staying over at each other's house. Nick's mom was the best cook I'd ever met and I tried to stay over at his house as much as possible. Their evening meals were plentiful, with fried chicken, sweet corn, potatoes, salad and dessert. I just loved eating over at Nick's house! Mrs. G's meals were a far cry from the macaroni and cheese, fish sticks and creamed corn from a can that my family ate for dinner most nights, but I would never tell my mom how much better the food was at Nick's house. I wonder if she knew...

My dad would get three weeks of vacation a year from his newspaper job. During those three weeks he would pack up the family and visit places. We didn't have money for hotels, so we'd go camping. It was a blast! When I was six years old my dad packed up some of us kids and drove back to East

St. Louis to visit my grandpa and Uncle Evarist. After that, it was off to Chicago to visit some aunts, then to Minneapolis to visit my dad's parents. We took our Ford station wagon with two racks on the roof spilling over with our luggage, sleeping bags and a tent. We completed the 1800-mile round trip with no problems. I'd never met some of the relatives before, so the trip left an impression. Every family should take a long road trip like that. It created bonds and lifelong memories.

What made the trip even more memorable was that it happened before the Interstate Highway System was constructed. That meant we traveled on two-lane highways, passing through small towns along the way. I never knew there were that many small towns! To get through the day without fighting, we'd play games as we traveled, read books, slept, prayed the rosary and played our favorite game, "Letting out Frankie." This would likely be illegal today, but Frankie was a rag we tied to the end of a long string that we would let out the window when traffic was light.

We would watch as Frankie flopped along the highway behind our car, twirling in the wind, up and down off the black top road. When we got close to a town or nearing traffic, my dad would tell us to "Bring in Frankie," at which point we'd reel him in until the next long stretch of light traffic. Throughout the trip we went through a number of Frankies and balls of string. Another kick we enjoyed was pumping our arms up and down when we passed large trucks to get the truck drivers to blow their truck horn. About half of the truck drivers gave us the thrill with a good long air blast. I wonder if that still works with truckers?

When we reached our respective destinations, my dad pitched our tent so we could sleep outdoors. It was something to sleep outside at night while being surrounded by my family. A kid couldn't feel safer.

At my grandpa's farm in East St. Louis and at my grandparents' home in Minneapolis we pitched the tent in their back yards and camped out. My parents slept in the house. In Minneapolis, we would go to Lake Minnetonka, one of the larger lakes of the state of "10,000 Lakes," just west of Minneapolis. We spent time fishing, boating, swimming and having fun hanging out with each other. If there was a water sport we could participate in, we'd do it. We loved our summer trips, but we only took two long road trips together.

Our normal getaway was to California for a week or two, where we'd camp out, usually at O'Neill's Park in Trabuco Canyon in southern California. The campground was centrally located for us, which was important. That way we could go to Disneyland, Knott's Berry Farm and the beautiful California beaches. Sometimes we'd head to Northern Arizona to camp near Sedona, Camp Verde, Flagstaff, Oak Creek Canyon, Payson and the beautiful White Mountains. In the White Mountains near Show Low, Arizona, we'd camp out and go fishing at Hawley Lake for fresh mountain lake trout.

On several occasions we caught our limit and ate trout for breakfast, lunch and dinner. When we weren't fishing, my dad took us on hikes in the forest or horseback riding.

On Labor Day we would go to the R & G Ranch in East Phoenix, a recreational facility sponsored by my father's work for its employees and their families. The ranch was neat; it had a swimming pool, a shuffleboard court, ping-pong tables, a clubhouse with a pool table and plenty of picnic areas where the families could barbeque. It also had a train that weaved through the orange groves of the property that we would ride and enjoy.

My dad didn't believe in wasting a day of his vacation. He got us out of the Phoenix summer heat whenever he could. It was a blast to blow up our air mattresses, unroll our sleeping bags, set up camp and sleep in the wilderness. My mother always slept on a cot near the entrance of the tent because some of us kids occasionally walked in our sleep. With my mother at the entrance of the tent she made sure none of her little cubs wandered away from the campsite in the dead of night. At a Boy Scout Camporee, when I was around 12 years old, I did that. I walked in my sleep right out of my two-man pup tent and into another troop's campsite a few hundred yards away. When I woke I remember my panic and the embarrassment. From then on I never really slept well when I went camping.

While my summers were mixed with work and vacation, there was nothing better than a Halloween, Thanksgiving,

Christmas and Easter at the Raths' house. Halloween was when brother Ron and I would go for the gusto. With some old raggedy clothes, which weren't hard to find in our house, and a charred cork to paint our cheeks black, we went out at sunset for candy dressed as bums. Empty pillowcases in hand, we ran door to door for about four hours to get as much candy as possible. At the end of the night and totally exhausted, we would get home with the now full pillowcases over our shoulders and pour the candy out on the living room carpet. Bonanza!! Wow. What a feast!! Every kind of candy on the planet was laid out on the floor. Then came the haggling between the two of us... "I'll give you two Mars bars for one box of Dots"... and on and on until we were satisfied with our respective stash of candy. Mother then would come in the room and put a damper on everything when she told us we needed to give 25% of our candy to the poor. "Poor!!! That would be me," I thought. But, this allowed me to get rid of the candy I couldn't pawn off to Ron, black licorice and jawbreakers, and still look like a sweet, generous kid.

Thanksgiving was a big spread of turkey and all the trimmings at Aunt Rita and Uncle Bob's house. We would pile into the station wagon and arrive with empty stomachs ready to be filled with Rita's great cooking. She was on par with Mrs. Ganem when it came to preparing a great meal. After dinner we would play with our three cousins, Jim, Marie and Peggy, in their back yard well into the evening. I look back on these times with delight when I realize how fortunate I was to have been surrounded by such a large and loving family who believed in celebrating holidays together.

At Christmas, all of us Raths kids decorated the tree in our front room, hung up the lights on the outside of the house and wrapped gifts to put under the tree. By Christmas morning there was little space to walk in our living room. I would have trouble sleeping Christmas Eve, because I was so anxious to see my gifts from Santa Claus. This was one time of year that my mother broke open the bank account and splurged. She made sure we all received a nice gift or two. Before we could open any of our gifts on Christmas morning we all had to go to Mass. My mother stressed the real meaning of Christmas, so we all went to the first Mass of the day at 7:00 in the morning. We couldn't wait for the final song at Mass, Joy to the World. After that last note, we'd rush home to open our gifts. Aunt Rita, Uncle Bob and the cousins would come over later in the day for a big Christmas feast of ham, yams, green beans and pumpkin pie. Mom saved up to create that delicious spread!

The next big holiday for us was Easter, which was not just a day to celebrate the resurrection of Jesus Christ, but for us kids, when we got a strong whiff of vinegar in the house, we rushed to the breakfast room table to die hard-boiled eggs. Mom poured warm vinegar into cereal bowls and added the colored die, and then we would begin the annual ritual of dunking eggs into the colored vinegar until they bore the respective color. After Easter dinner, mom would hide the eggs in the backyard for the Easter egg hunt. We Raths kids, plus our cousins, would grab an empty basket and run into the backyard to find the hidden eggs. Fun was had by all! Inevitably, months later we would find a rotten egg in the oleander bushes that we missed on Easter Sunday.

CHAPTER 11

At age 11, when I was in the fifth grade, I became an altar boy and began to serve Mass at St. Gregory's Church. This was difficult for me because all the prayers in 1964 were still in Latin, and to become an altar boy I had to learn the prayers in Latin. After several weeks of studying the language I served my first Mass for the church pastor, Monsignor Gordon. My heart swelled with pride at the end of that Mass! No one knew how hard I had practiced to get the prayers right. The priest in charge of the altar boys was a stickler about not missing assignments. If an altar boy missed his assignment to serve Mass, he had to come to early morning 6:30 Mass for a week and sit at the side of the altar. This discipline was significant as a learning tool, because I learned not to miss or be late for any obligation.

Attending a Catholic grade school meant I wore a school uniform. I didn't know it then, but I was being prepared to wear a uniform later in life. At St. Gregory's the boys wore tan pants with a white shirt and polished shoes. Our hair had to be cut nicely and we had to be well groomed. The girls wore blue plaid skirts and white blouses, with their black-and-white saddle Oxfords and bobby socks. Every recess in the earlier grades, we boys played marbles in the dirt of the schoolyard.

On a good day, I managed to increase the size of my marble bag with a few cat eyes, boulders, clearies and steelies. On a bad day, I'd go home a little light in the bag.

My days at St. Gregory have brought with them many memories. One I'll never forgot. It was in November of 1963. It was a clear, crisp day as I walked out of the school's cafeteria and onto the playground. Something was in the air. I couldn't figure out what was going on. I noticed several children hovering around Sister Sylvester near the swing sets, so I began to walk toward them. As I grew closer, I heard chatter from the kids that Kennedy had been shot. My first thought was do we have a student named Kennedy? Who got shot? Then one of my friends turned to me and said that President Kennedy was shot in Dallas. My heart sank. Kennedy was the first Catholic President of the United States and was very popular with the students of our school. We were told to go back to our classrooms. We didn't know that Kennedy had lost his life. We proceeded to the church where we said the rosary for our wounded President. Only later did we learn that he had died of gunshot wounds while proceeding in a motorcade through the streets of Dallas. That was November 22nd, 1963.

After school I ran home and watched the television coverage of the event. Our whole family seemed glued to the television for several hours that night. We didn't want to believe what we were seeing and hearing… our beloved President was dead, and Vice President Johnson took the oath of office on Air

Force One just before leaving Love Field in Dallas on his way back to Washington, D.C.

The adored Jackie Kennedy looked so sad in her black veil with her two young children, John and Caroline, at her side during the nationally broadcasted events leading to President Kennedy's funeral on November 25th. On the Sunday after the assassination, the slain President's flag-draped coffin was carried on a horse-drawn caisson to the U.S. Capitol to lie in state. Throughout the day and night in the cold weather, hundreds of thousands of citizens lined up to view the guarded casket. Representatives from countries around the world attended the state funeral. After the Requiem Mass at St. Matthew's Cathedral, the late President was buried at Arlington National Cemetery in Virginia, where an eternal flame burns to this day in his honor.

Just the year prior, in February 1962, the entire nation was celebrating the American astronaut John Glenn's space flight around the earth. This was an important achievement, because when Kennedy began his presidency in 1961 it was his vision to send a man to the moon before the end of the decade. It was during this time that I became interested in the space program.

CHAPTER 12

I started watching and keeping track of all the manned space flights. I kept a scrapbook with pictures of the space capsules and large rocket ships blasting off from their launch pads from Cape Kennedy (originally called Cape Canaveral). In my sixth-grade science class I learned about rocket and jet propulsion and the effects of space on the human body. I couldn't get enough of the space program and the "jet age." My interest in jets and military history set me on a path to becoming a top fighter pilot later in life. It was my destiny and I embraced it.

I always asked my dad about his flying adventures in World War II, and I went through all of his photographs he had kept from the war. He didn't share a lot about his war experiences, as was true of many veterans of that war. Most veterans of that time just wanted to get back to a normal life with their families and leave the hell of war behind them. My dad did let me put up a montage of pictures of him, his A-20 crewmembers and other war photos on the wall in our hallway. I titled the collection Dad's Army Pictures.

Luke Air Force Base is west of Phoenix and dad would take us kids to air shows at the base. I loved going to the shows and appreciated all the different military aircraft in the U.S.

arsenal. I loved to watch as the pilots would perform their death-defying stunts in the air. The deep blue skies over the base provided a playground for these dare devils to entertain the large crowd. "Wow, I wanna do that!" I told my dad as my eyes followed the pilots' maneuvers in the air above us.

He replied, "You'd make a great pilot, Son."

After the air show dad took us to Litchfield Park, a graveyard for thousands of World War II aircraft that were parked there to die. At the end of the war and with the downsizing of the U.S. military, they were no longer useful. "What a shame, what a shame," I remember saying. These wartime beauties looked like fallen angels with nowhere to go as they baked in the Arizona sun with the hope that someone may come along and restore them to their proud glory days. Most went to the scrap yard, but a few survived and still fly today, equipped with their proud paintjobs and flown by some crusty old pilots.

Later in life, on my father's 90th birthday, we kids paid for our dad to fly in a restored B-17 Flying Fortress that was flown out of Falcon Field in Mesa, Arizona. As he got out of the plane after an hour-long flight over the Arizona skies, all he could say was, "Dang that thing was loud," referring to the noisy four engines that powered this strategic World War II bomber. Also, on the flight was another passenger, a pretty young blonde girl wearing tight shorts.

My dad said with his usual smile, "I don't recall girls like that on my combat missions over Germany." We all laughed!

Back to my childhood...

On Sunday evenings our family would gather around the television and watch The Ed Sullivan Show, Candid Camera and Bonanza. Television was becoming more and more a part of every family's life. Ed Sullivan introduced some amazing new talent of that day, like The Beatles.

In February 1964, word spread about a young English band of four young men with long hair who'd be playing on the Ed Sullivan Show. We all sat down and watched this crazy night of television as The Beatles performed live on the show. We boys thought it was hilarious to watch as the young girls in the audience screamed and fainted. My dad couldn't figure out what all the fuss was about. Elvis Presley had been the big name in music at the time, but the Beatles took over the music charts with hit after hit. It was exciting to see the rock-and-roll revolution come into full swing. I'm proud to say I was there to see it happen.

The Beatles paved the way for other groups, like The Beach Boys, The Rolling Stones, The Doors, Gary Pucket and the Union Gap, and then all the Motown sensations. Music had changed for good, and I was right in the middle of it.

In 1968, Nick and I won tickets from a local radio show to see The Doors in concert at Veterans Coliseum in Phoenix. We were just 15, but we threw our hippie beads around our necks, jumped on our bikes and pedaled to the show. What a wild and crazy November night. Jim Morrison and the band were out of control. At the end of the concert, when they played their hit song, Light My Fire, hundreds of fans stormed the stage to touch Morrison. I watched in shock and awe as police officers tried to restore order, but couldn't. Utter chaos ensued and the lights were turned on. It was the end of the party. Everyone was ordered to leave the building. After that, The Doors were forever banned from playing in Phoenix.

To top off our night of wild abandon, Nick and I met two girls at the show. We hung out with them till the police issued their mandate for everyone to leave the premises. The girls asked for a ride home, but we only had our bicycles. We were able to get their phone numbers and ended up taking them to the movies at a later date.

I couldn't wait to get my driver's license. Just one more year!

CHAPTER 13

As a young teenager I would ride in my brother's car and cruise Central Avenue in Phoenix, with the local radio stations KRIZ or KRUX turned up at a high volume. In that time, cars would line the avenue in parking lots with their hoods up to show off their powerful V8 engines and 4-barrel carburetors, not to mention the fancy paint schemes on their rides. It was a great time in our country's history to be a teenager. This was right out of Happy Days.

Unfortunately, over the next few years many rock and roll icons suffered premature deaths. Jimi Hendricks died in 1970, Jim Morrison of the Doors in 1971, Mama Cass Elliot of the Mamas and the Papas in 1974, the great Elvis Presley in 1977, and Beatle John Lennon was gunned down in New York in December of 1980. The illegal drug epidemic was in full swing and many musicians found themselves strung out on drugs which led to several early deaths. I was determined to stay away from drugs even though marijuana was coming into my community for the first time. I had goals to reach and I needed a clear head, so I never let the temptation cross my lips.

When it came time to choose a high school, I realized that I had no desire to go to the seminary. This was not a big deal for my family. Both of my brothers had since left the seminary during their senior year and returned to local Catholic high schools. Bob went to St. Mary's Catholic High School in Phoenix where he graduated, and Steve went to Bishop Bourgade High School in Phoenix. My sister, Jean, given the name Sister Mary St. Jane, would leave the convent after her first vows. She met a medical student, Jonathan Costa, in Chicago and they got married in 1971 and raised four wonderful children.

I'm somewhat surprised by how my mother took all of these events. She wasn't upset. As a matter of fact, she made sure we all knew that she only wanted what was best for us. If we weren't happy in seminary school, so be it. With that, my brother, Ron, went to Bourgade High School. I followed him in September 1967. With finances stressed at home, I had to pay for some of my high school tuition and books, which wasn't a problem for me. Nick decided to attend Bourgade, too, as did many of my friends from St. Gregory's. I was a happy camper!

With Boy Scouts officially behind me, I was ready for the big times ahead. I had sprouted up to almost 6 feet tall by the time I entered high school, but I was skinny. In order to play high school sports I had to gain weight and muscle, so I started working out at the local gym with Nick. We had one goal: to bulk up. It was a race.

Bourgade was a small school of only about 650 students. My freshman class had 145 students, with most of the students coming from the Catholic elementary schools in the area. The school was taught by the Marist priests and IBVM nuns. My class was the fifth graduating class, as the school was relatively new.

St. Gregory's school ran a school bus to Bourgade, which made it easy for me to get to school. Otherwise, I'd have to bike the four miles it took to get there. The distance meant I'd have to be quicker to rise in the morning and better prepare for my day. The days of rolling out of bed, getting dressed and walking across the street to my school were over.

Although grade school was great for me, my high school days were four of the best years of my life. Stumbling through the first few weeks was awkward, but I soon settled into a routine and high school life. I tried out for football for the freshman team, but with only 18 of us trying out we all made the team. Our coach asked us to write down the position we wanted to play. I watched him jot notes down on his clipboard. I was last to select a position. No one had selected the position of center, so I picked center and became an immediate starter on the team. Little did I know at the time that our freshman football coach, Mr. Heward, had no experience coaching football. He was a biologist, not a coach. We went through our daily practices after school in the Arizona heat preparing for our first game. We learned new plays, conducted tackling drills, attacked the dummy sled and bulked up pumping weights. I'm guessing that Coach Heward had to study up on the drills.

Finally, our first game arrived. The cheerleaders milled about as they prepared their cheer routines, the field was lined with chalk, the scoreboard was turned on and a few spectators came to watch us take the field on a warm Thursday afternoon. In the locker room before the game the coach handed us our game jerseys. I will never forget those ugly burlap-sack brown jerseys. They should have been blue and tan, the school's colors. To this day I don't know what happened.

To make things worse the coach threw me my game jersey with the number 22 scrolled across the back. My number should have a number from 50 to 59, because I was the offensive center and defensive linebacker. I wasn't the only one who was confused. All the team members complained openly about their numbers, because they didn't make sense. Finally a player spoke up.

"Coach, you have all the numbers mixed up for each specific position," a player said.

The coach replied, "It doesn't matter what number you wear."

We all looked at each other. Oh, no, we thought as one mind. Coach doesn't even know what numbers we should wear. This is not good. If he doesn't know this basic fact about football, what else doesn't he know?

Everything went downhill from there. The game was a disaster with a grueling loss of 45-0. My big debut of high school football was a calamity. Our team never got the ball across the 50-yard line. The coach berated us after the game calling us "nothing but a bunch of sh*t birds."

The season was an absolute failure. We lost every game and never even scored a single point. Before our last game our teachers told us we would not have homework for a week if we only scored a point, a single point. In our defense, we managed to drive the ball to the 20-yard line on our final possession and with fourth down we set up for a field goal, even though we were losing 37-0. The stands grew quiet as I snapped the ball to Nick, the holder, who set the ball down and our kicker, Johnny Aguilera, booted the ball toward the goal posts, only to have it veer off to the right and short. The missed kick was an appropriate end to our dismal season. It was time to throw in the jersey for the season!

CHAPTER 14

Fortunately, there was more to high school than football. I enjoyed my freshman year, taking college prep classes in English, Algebra and Spanish. I made new friends and I fit into my new environment with amazing ease. To think that I'd been nervous!

In October I ran for class President. My biggest competitor was Ken Groom, a friend from St. Gregory's, who was the frontrunner. He was well respected among the students and faculty members, and he would be a huge challenge for me. I had a way with the girls and slowly made progress getting their votes. On Election Day, I squeaked out a narrow victory. I thoroughly enjoyed leading my class throughout the school year of 1967-1968, along with our Vice President Marcia Popik.

In January 1968, our school sponsored a bus trip to Flagstaff, Arizona and the Snow Bowl. The Snow Bowl is a winter resort for skiing, snow tubing and a great place to have fun in the snow. I had never seen snow, so I was very excited to play in the snow with my classmates. I recall looking out the bus window as we got to the higher elevations and into the tall pines and snow. What a magnificent sight. The pine trees were draped with snow, pulling down the branches with its weight.

The drive up to the Snow Bowl was also special when some of us in the far back of the bus decided to play the kissing game, spin the bottle. We had several willing players, including some of the best-looking girls in our class. I waited patiently for that bottle to stop spinning when Kathy Wilkinson made her spin. She was the hot blonde we all wanted to kiss. I finally got that chance when her spin of the bottle faced me. Playing in the snow the rest of the day did not compare to that special kiss with Kathy. By the end of the day we were all wet, exhausted and asleep on the bus as we made our way back down to Phoenix.

In the spring it was baseball season and I was ready to take the diamond. Our team looked pretty good overall and we even had a coach that knew a little bit about baseball. I played first base and took the number 7 after the great Mickey Mantle. Our team had a respectable season with more wins than loses. All those years of summer baseball paid off as I hit over .350 for the season.

Even with all the sports, not all days were filled with fun and games. In April 1968, I was walking up the stairs to one of my classes when a fellow student asked me if I heard the news that the Reverend Martin Luther King, Jr., had been assassinated. The prominent leader of the civil rights movement was assassinated at the Lorraine Motel in Memphis, Tennessee, on April 4, 1968, at the age of 39. James Earl Ray, a fugitive from the Missouri State Penitentiary, was arrested and charged with the crime. He entered a plea of guilty and was sentenced to 99 years in the Tennessee State Penitentiary. Ray would die in prison at the age of 70.

The year 1968 was difficult for America's best and brightest. This year took another ugly turn when on June 6th Senator Robert "Bobby" Kennedy (NY), the brother of John F. Kennedy, was assassinated at the Ambassador Hotel in Los Angeles, California. He and his wife Ethel were there to celebrate his winning the Presidential primary for California. He was just 42 years old. The killer was arrested and identified as Sirhan Sirhan, a Christian Arab from Jordan, who is now serving a life sentence for the senator's murder. I know I don't have to give these details herein, but they were important to me. In fact, my interest in politics may have started with these tragedies. How could I affect change? That became a driving force in my life, and it may be why I enjoyed working in the White House later in life.

I was becoming an adult during troubled times in our country's history. Of course, I didn't know that at the time. I was just living my life, entering a path and walking with friends toward an uncertain future. When I finished my freshman year in May 1968 the war in Vietnam was escalating. Thousands of U.S. troops arrived every day to fight the North Vietnamese communist guerillas and Viet Cong. There were over 536,000 American troops fighting the war with little progress being made, which led President Johnson to forego another run for the presidency that year.

There were anti-war riots during the Democratic National Party Convention in Chicago, where hundreds of demonstrators were arrested. When the Presidential election of 1968 was over and the votes tallied, Richard M. Nixon became our nation's 37th President, defeating Minnesota's Hubert Humphrey. I will remember 1968 as a very sad year of my life. Strike that! It was a terrible year for everyone in the country when it came to national turmoil, assassinations and chaos. I was glad to see 1969 arrive. I was then a sophomore at Bourgade and we just finished the junior varsity football season with no wins, but we did manage to score a few points throughout the season.

During my sophomore and junior years I stayed out of school politics and concentrated on my studies and sports. I did co-chair our Junior/Senior prom at a local Phoenix hotel, however. We knew our time in high school would end soon and we'd have to choose a real path in life, but for now we were intent on having fun. That included attending our prom and class dances. Enough said.

When I was a sophomore, my parents were asked by the Catholic Relief Society to take in a foreign exchange student from Brazil. He was my age, and my mother asked me to be his sponsor while he lived with us. I was reluctant to have him live with us, since I already had all my friends. I gave in and Servulo Resende, a 15-year-old boy who came from a very wealthy family in San Paulo, briefly joined our family. It ended up being more of a shock to his lifestyle than to ours. Servulo was used to servants and housekeepers, and he found it a surprise when he saw our tight living quarters at our house. He learned our lifestyle and tried his best to blend in, and at school he assimilated quite well with the other students. He lived with us for nine months before he returned to Brazil, where he went on to become a very successful physician.

During that year I had my own lawn service and mowed several lawns a week for income. My dad bought me a trailer for my lawn gear, and my mom would tow the trailer to my customers' homes. I remember unhooking the trailer so she could go back home with the car. This way I mowed several lawns in the neighborhood and then later she would pick me up and take me to the next neighborhood. On some days I would mow over ten lawns earning $5 a piece, netting me over $50 a day.

I played summer American Legion baseball to keep my baseball skills sharp for high school ball. By mid-season we were having a phenomenal year, and on July 20, 1969, we faced our most challenging opponent of the season. This game would determine if we moved ahead into the summer playoffs.

Earlier that week, Apollo 11 had blasted off from Cape Kennedy on its way to the moon with Neil Armstrong, Buzz Aldrin and Michael Collins. Everyone was pegged to the television waiting for the moment they landed on the moon and begin their moon walk. Unfortunately, the moon landing was scheduled for the exact time of my ball game, and I was torn between watching the moon landing or playing in the baseball game. I decided to play in the ball game, since I had committed to the sport and all its practices and games when I joined the league. The lesson I learned early in life to stick to my commitments helped me make the right decision. I was able to see the moon landing on several replays that evening and we did win the ballgame. In fact, we made it into the playoffs.

By the time my 16th birthday rolled around on September 12, 1969, I was ready to get my driver's license, so on my birthday my dad took me to the DMV where I took the written and driving tests, and was cleared to take to the roadways. The problem now was that my parents owned one car and there were now several drivers in the family, so it was going to be difficult to get the car for dating or other activities.

As a high school junior, I played on the varsity football team with the more experienced seniors, one being my brother Ron, and we were finally winning games. Coaches Fenton and Abels knew the sport well, and led us to a four-win/ six-loss season. I played both offense and defense, and at the end of the season I was named honorable mention to the all-conference team, along with three other players.

At the end of the football season Mr. Abels was looking to

sell his sweet 1967 Firebird, with a 440 engine and four on the floor. I had $1,600 in my bank account and I was ready to buy a car. I didn't need a loan, I didn't need my parents help to pay for the car, and I wanted this muscle car. Mr. Abels let me take it for a spin one afternoon, and when I turned on the engine and drove away, it took off like a rocket ship.

My buddy, Dave Bruchhauser, pulled up next to me at a stoplight on Camelback Road in his 1966 Pontiac GTO, and we both revved the engines as we waited for the light to turn green. When the light turned we both laid rubber for over 50 feet until the tires stuck to the pavement and within a few seconds we both were over 60 mph. Damn, I want this car! That's all I could think about. The price tag? Just $1,500. I'd have money left over for gas, insurance and extras. All I had to do was to convince my father that this car was ready for me and I was ready for the car.

I slowly pulled up to my house in the Firebird late in the afternoon knowing my father would be home. I parked the car in the driveway and went into the house and got my dad. We both walked out and he took a good look at the Firebird and said, "What's this?"

I said, "This is the car I want to buy." I told him I had the money in the bank, but I wanted his permission.

"Well, let's take it for a drive," he said.

"Get in and let's do this," I replied, all full of youthful

bravado.

I slowly drove away from our house on Whitton Avenue as I shifted into second gear, then third, then fourth. My dad told me to look at the speedometer and I was already at 40 mph in a 25 mph residential zone, so I quickly downshifted to third, but it was too late. My dad told me to take the car back home. I pulled up into our driveway and killed the engine. We both sat there quietly as I waited for what I knew was coming next.

My dad said, "Son, I know you have the money to buy the car, but for your own safety and well-being I cannot give you my blessing to go ahead with the purchase."

Maybe I wasn't like other kids, but at that moment I knew I wasn't going to change his mind and accepted his decision. I drove the car back to Mr. Abels' place. At least for a couple of days I enjoyed the satisfaction of driving one of the best muscle cars of all time. It would take me a long time to realize that my father was likely right. Maybe if I had kept that car I may have done something foolish like racing with friends and lost my life. I may not have gotten involved in school politics again and I may have gone a different route altogether in life. One never knows. I have children of my own now, and I completely understand my father's position. When my son turned 16, I sold my Mazda RX-7 sports car for the exact same reason.

CHAPTER 15

I was ready to get involved in school politics again, so I ran for class President of my senior class. My rival, Ken Groom, went on to run for student body President. We both won and worked together to make our final school year, 1970-1971, a great year. I buckled down with my studies as I prepared for college. My math teacher, Father Jim Rodenspiel, kept the fire in my belly burning for mathematics. I would need a lot of math in my future. Father Rodenspiel was my mentor and pushed me hard in algebra, trigonometry and calculus, and he became my sponsor for the National Honor Society. With his sponsorship I was awarded membership my senior year. I was on my way to a successful future without realizing it. Later Father Rodenspiel would die of cancer and I found a way to get to Coeur d'Alene, Idaho, where he had been living for his funeral. In his will he requested I be one of his pallbearers, and he left me a picture of him and me where he wrote, "Greg, go after your dreams; life is short and never look back, make me proud." Those words made me even more determined to be a success in life.

My senior year in high school was my best year ever at this point in my life. Summer training began early for the football season. We had a new head coach, Mr. Bill Maas. An intelligent man who knew the game well and wanted us to be winners, Coach Maas developed a new offense and a defense that stacked linebackers on the offensive center for multiple blitzes. We were well prepared for our first game and were decked out in our new blue and tan jerseys with blue helmets. We felt like a million bucks.

Our helmets had a jet on each side signifying our school mascot, The Blue Angels, the Navy's Flight Demonstration team. It is coincidental that five years later I would be flying that exact same jet that was on my helmet. Our first opponent was a home game against a highly regarded team from Blythe, California. We were definitely the underdogs by a wide margin. Before the game several of us players shaved our heads as a show of solidarity and school spirit. It wasn't easy to shave off my blonde locks, but I caved under peer pressure, and like my younger years, my hair laid on the floor once again. I didn't take my helmet off the entire game, even when my Aunt Rita in the stands yelled for me to do it, because she'd heard a rumor and wanted to see if it was true. It took some time for my hair to grow back. Ah, youth…

I was voted captain of the team and called the defensive plays. The other captain was Nick, who was our quarterback, calling the offensive plays. We had a strong front line and a tough running game led by our running backs, Jimmy O'Connor, Mike Kelly and Chet Garry. Our first game began with all the fanfare of the first home game of the season, the bleachers were full, and the cheerleaders and pompom girls were decked out in the blue outfits. We left the locker room and ran out onto the lit field crashing through the paper barrier held by the cheerleaders. We were pumped! This was going to be a great season!

The game was hard hitting throughout the first half and we went into half time tied at 6-6. At half time Coach Maas and assistant Coach Abels pumped us up even more. The third quarter ended with us still deadlocked in the 6-6 tie. With only a couple of minutes left in the game, I was thinking that a final tie score was a good effort against this highly rated California team. Then came the play of the game, we had the ball on our own 14-yard line late in the fourth quarter and our running back, Jim O'Connor, took the ball from Nick and ran a sweep to the right side and ran 86 yards for the game winning touchdown. Coach Maas was on the sideline looking for a player for the next play when he heard the screaming and turned around to see Jimmy streaking up the right sideline. We won the game 12-6 and the crowd went crazy in the bleachers!

We would win the next four games, and by midseason the same group of kids that never scored a point freshman year was now ranked number one in the state of Arizona with a 5-0 record, outscoring our opponents 126-32. We ended the season with a final record of 7-3, losing two very close games. The other loss was a blowout by the score of 36-0 by the team that went on to win the state championship for 1970. Four of our players made the all-conference team and I was honored to have made the all-state team. In my yearbook Coach Maas wrote, "Greg, Many thanks for the great contribution you gave to the football team, you did an outstanding job and was rewarded for it. Don't ever hesitate to call me for anything. Good luck."

Coach made me feel great about my participation. With his simple words he taught me about the importance of recognizing people for outstanding work. I would use this in my life. I recently reconnected with Coach Maas and we have become good friends again. It was his excellence and knowledge of the game that took us to that next level. I had a chance to tell him that as an adult.

After the football games, if there wasn't a dance at school, my friends and I would drive to a place in the desert, north of Phoenix, where we would hang out. We called the place "the well," because there was a deep abandoned well that we circled with our cars, and then started a bonfire, had a couple beers that someone was able to bring and played music from our 8-track car stereo. The best part of the well was that we would toss the empty beer cans down the deep well to get rid of any evidence. One night, a classmate, Tom Keefe, pulled a prank on us. He had a red light that he put on the top of his car, and as he drove closer to us on the dirt road, we thought he was the cops, so we threw the beer down the well. Thanks, Tom. What a waste!

By midseason my hair was finally growing out and I asked a classmate, Kathy McMahon to the Homecoming dance. She was the best friend of Nick's sweetheart, Lori Hinnenkamp. Kathy was one of ten children, eight girls and two boys. With such large families we both had a lot in common. Senior year, we four became inseparable.

On October 9, 1970, our football team beat Tolleson High School by a score of 46-0. It was a huge victory for us. After the game we all went to the Village Inn Pizza Parlor to celebrate with our classmates. After pizza, Nick drove Lori, Kathy and me around in Lori's sister's car. The car was a 1967 Chevy Camaro, the muscle car of all muscle cars. I loved that thing. Once we got to Lori's house, Nick let me drive the car around the neighborhood with Kathy. As I was getting ready to head back for Lori's house, Kathy asked if she could take the wheel and take it for a short drive. Kathy didn't even have her driver's license, so I was hesitant to give her the wheel. Finally, after a kiss on my neck I agreed and we switched seats. It's amazing the power of a little kiss at that age. Kathy revved the Camaro up and took off down a main street until she came to an intersection into a residential neighborhood where she made a sharp left turn and lost control. The back end slipped from under us and we headed straight toward a light pole.

"Hit the brakes!" I screamed, reaching over and grabbing the wheel.

But it was too late. We smashed straight into the utility power pole, knocking out power to the entire neighborhood. Neither of us was injured, but steam rose from the ruptured radiator and fluids pooled under the car. We got out and stared at the damage. I couldn't believe this had just happened.

What should we say? I had a license; Kathy didn't. Kathy hit the pole; I didn't. I should never have let Kathy drive the car. Kathy quickly took the high road and said she would accept the blame. Within a few minutes a squad car was on the scene. Two officers took our stories and Kathy was cited for reckless driving and driving without a license. A tow truck took the car away, and Kathy and I were put in the back seat of the squad car. They would drop us off at Lori's house. We'd been gone a long time and Lori and Nick were freaking out. After the police drove away we told Nick and Lori the whole story as they listened in total shock. I dreaded the next part; we had to tell Lori's sister that we crashed her Camaro. I was sick to my stomach. To say Karen was upset is an understatement. Kathy's parents were also disappointed in both of us, but they never told my parents. We could smile about the "wreck" later, but I really don't think Karen has ever forgiven us for crashing her sweet ride. It never drove the same after all the repairs.

In January 1971, it was time again for our annual Snow Bowl trip to Flagstaff. Several of us seniors went on the trip, but before we loaded onto the bus, Nick showed me a bottle of Jim Beam in his coat pocket. Off we went for a day of fun and "drinking" in the snow. We arrived and soon a few of us guys went into the woods to take a swig of the Jim Beam. We passed the bottle around and when it got to me the third time, the guys all started chanting, "Chug, chug, chug! Come on, Greg, chug it all down."

That's all it took to make me do something dumb. I lay down on my back in the snow and finished off the bottle. I got up feeling good and smiled as we made our way back to the main slope where our classmates were snow tubing down the snow covered hills. Things were suddenly blurry. The mountains seemed to be moving, and I was seeing double. I'm gonna hurl, I thought, and ran back into the woods. Nick came to my aid and found my situation rather amusing, but was concerned that a chaperone may find me in this state. Nick was not much better himself, but he wasn't vomiting. We were near the main assembly area looking for a bathroom when one of the nuns from our school noticed what was going on. She knew immediately we were both drunk, so she made us sit on the bus for the rest of the day to sober up. Once the sun had set it was time to head back for Phoenix. I was absolutely miserable, my head was pounding and I was shaking uncontrollably. As I tried to focus I noticed everyone was sleeping from all the fun, and here I was sick as a dog from the whisky.

When the bus arrived back at the school, the now-sober Nick drove me home. When we got to my house he helped me through the back door, gave me a couple aspirins and helped me into bed. When Nick was ready to make his way out of my bedroom and out of the house, my dad walked in and asked Nick what was wrong with me.

"I think he has the flu or something," Nick replied as he hurried past my father and out to his car. That story worked until the following Monday when the Dean of Students called my parents and alerted them of my actions at the Snow Bowl. My parents were not at all happy, but I think they knew that this would be a good learning experience. The next morning, Nick and I, and our parents were sitting in the Dean's Office awaiting the punishment. The Dean handed out our punishments of after-school work, and I lost my phone privileges at home for a month. I would miss my evening calls to Kathy.

All the stupidity behind me, I was ready for baseball season, which began with two losses out of our first three games. That's okay. We ended strong, winning 14 of the next 17 games, though we did miss the playoffs. We had tied for first place with Tolleson High School, but we both missed the state playoffs when a team from another division got the nod for the state tournament. All and all it was a very successful year for all of our sports teams. Late in April 1971, I received a letter from Frank Kush, the head football coach at Arizona State University, congratulating me for making the all-state football team and he told me not to sign with any other college team until he talked with me. Unfortunately, I never got the call and I hung up my football shoes for the time being. Now that I wouldn't be playing college sports I had to figure out what I was going to do in my life.

As my high school days came to a close, I attended the senior prom with Kathy, and Nick took Lori. On May 27, 1971, 133 of us seniors walked across the stage to receive our high school diplomas. A great time of my life had come to an end. I looked at the row of graduates in our blue and gold caps and gowns knowing I may never see many of these people again. It was sad as this chapter in my life closed. That night many of us stayed up until sunrise. It was the climax of four great years.

I had taken my SATs and ACTs, earning average scores. An academic scholarship was not happening. With my parents having little money to pay for my college, I decided to go to Phoenix Community College for my first two years. The summer after high school was an active one for me. I ran my lawn service and prepared for college.

Not attending college was never an option in my family. My parents stressed that we all go to get a degree. My high school classmates were going their own ways to different colleges and universities, and the ol' high school gang was slowly breaking up. Kathy and I drifted apart. Kathy went to work full time and I started college. We saw little of each other once college started. Nick and Lori stayed together and got married in April of 1974.

CHAPTER 16

September 12, 1971, was not only my 18th birthday, but was my first day of college. I majored in business and took a full load of classes. I found college classes to be stimulating, but I missed the comradery of all my high school friends. Nick went to Phoenix College with me, so it was good to see him around campus. There were several Vietnam veterans in my classes, flipping their long hair over their shoulders and espousing pretty bitter attitudes. The returning veterans were not treated well by the American public and there were no homecoming parades or national support, which was sad to see after all they went through in Southeast Asia. Many of the veterans dropped out of college after a few weeks of classes. Looking back, I can see this happening. I understand it, especially now that I myself am a veteran. It must have been heartbreaking for them to return to a disgruntled public who didn't appreciate the efforts of these veterans.

I plugged along with college receiving average grades and found the transition to college rather smooth. I missed playing football, but I didn't have time for it since I took on another job at the local drugstore, Smith Osborn Pharmacy, working as a stock boy and cashier. I still worked my lawn jobs, but work was slow in the winter months. I didn't own a car, and with my savings dwindling, I bought a small Honda motorcycle. My mother was not at all happy that I bought a motorcycle, but she couldn't say much since I was now 18. My dad loved my bike and drove it when he could. He had a bike as a teenager and confided in me that he loved the thrill he got from riding a motorcycle. He ended up buying a motorcycle that same year.

With the war in Vietnam still raging, the Defense Department went to the lottery system in 1970. The lottery date for my birth year was on February 2, 1972. My birthday drew the number 43, and Nick's birthday drew 287. Nick was relieved, but I had to figure out my future, and soon. Although I had no problem joining the service, I wanted to finish college first. I didn't see my number coming up until later in the summer of that year, which gave me some time to think about what to do. A good friend, Eddie VanDerWerf, received a low number, so he joined the National Guard before the Army called him up. At the time we called the National Guard "Nixon's Girls," since it was considered a less than reputable military organization compared to the Regular Army or Marines, but it was a good move for Eddie to stay out of the war.

In the summer of 1972, with a year of college under my belt, I was at a friend's house for a swim party. Her name was Melissa Adams. Melissa's father owned a Buick dealership and had a nice home with a backyard swimming pool. There were about 20 of us swimming, carrying on and having a good time.

My friend from high school, Tom Keefe, was there and he was in a similar situation as I was when it came to the military lottery. He had done some investigating concerning military service and showed me some military brochures regarding the Marine Corps Officer Program. Tom wanted to be a military lawyer and I was interested in becoming a military pilot. The following day, August 12, 1972, we went down to the Marine Corps Officer Selection Office in downtown Phoenix to talk to the recruiters. After passing a battery of academic tests, a physical exam and an aviation aptitude exam I was sworn in as a Marine Corps Officer candidate. Tom also passed his tests and was sworn in with me.

My dad's work, the Phoenix Gazette newspaper, was across the street from the Marine Corps Officer Selection Office in downtown Phoenix, so Tom and I went to see him and told him the news. He was surprised to see us at his work and asked us what brought us to see him. I told him, "Dad, we joined the Marines!!"

"YOU DID WHAT?!" he exclaimed.

"Tom and I joined the Marine Officer Program," I replied. After a few minutes of silence, he told us he was excited for us, adding that it would be a difficult road ahead. He was right about that, but what this opportunity afforded me was to keep me out of the draft, gave me the incentive to complete college, and gave me the opportunity for a career in flying military aircraft.

Invaders from Mars.
The movie that scared me as a young child.

My parents, John and Viola Raths.
Wedding Day, Columbus, Mississippi, May 27, 1943.

Grandpa Alfred Raths, my parents,
Grandma Anna Raths, 1943.

My dad's A-20 Havoc with his crewmembers,
Sgt. Bill Albrecht and Sgt. Tom Oblak, England, 1944.

My mom and her sister Rita, and their father,
Grandpa Joseph Schwartz, 1944.

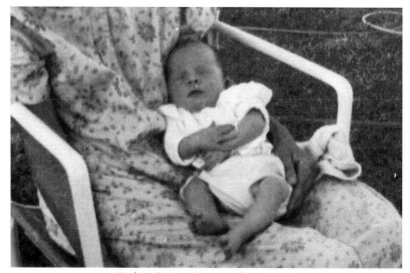

Baby Greg, September 1953.

My mom, and siblings Jean, Ron, Steve, me on my Aunt
Rita's lap, and brother Bob, 1954.

The home I grew up in Phoenix, 1808 W. Whitton Avenue,
and our 1956 Ford Station Wagon.

Ron, me, Bob and Steve at my grandparents' house
in Minneapolis, Minnesota, 1956.

At my Aunt Rita and Uncle Bob's Wedding,
November, 1958.

Aunt Rita, Steve, Ron and me, 1958.

Me and my brother Ron playing baseball in our
Phoenix home backyard, 1959.

My First Holy Communion at St. Gregory's Church,
Mom, me, Theresa, and Mary Ann, 1961.

Our favorite television show growing up,
The Wallace and Ladmo Show, 1962.

On a hike to Weaver's Needle deep into the
Superstition Mountains outside Phoenix, Steve, Ron,
and me, 1963.

Ron, Steve, me, Uncle Albert, Grandpa and Grandma Raths
in Minneapolis, Minnesota, 1966.

All the Raths' scouts. Standing: Ron and me; Sitting:
Bob, Dad, Mom, Steve; Kneeling: Mary Ann, Danny,
and Theresa, 1967.

Bourgade High School Football,
Coach Bill Maas and me, 1970.

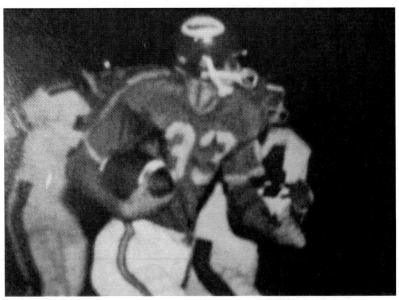

Our great running back at Bourgade High School,
Jimmy O'Connor #33, 1970.

Prom Night at Bourgade High School, Nick Ganem,
Lori Hinnenkamp, me and Kathy McMahon, 1971.

Bourgade High School Senior Class Officers, me, Carol Ford,
Dave Sanchez, and Regis Della-Calce, 1970-1971.

SECTION TWO

FROM TRAINING TO TAKE OFF:
MY TIME TO FLY!

The next few years of my life would be important. It was a
make-it-or-break-it point for me, and I knew it. I was entering
a military program that would determine my life's path,
no if's, and's or but's. Was I up to the challenge? What if I
couldn't hack it?

CHAPTER 17

The Marine Corps Officer Candidate Training Program I
signed on for consisted of two six-week summer sessions
in Quantico, Virginia. Upon college graduation I would be
commissioned a Marine Corps Officer. I wasn't obligated
for active military service until I received my commission
or dropped out of college. With an officer contract to be a
pilot I had to give the Marine Corps six years of my life after
flight training. I was very excited to know that I would have
creditable employment for several years after college. At the
time I signed up, there was a lot of anti-military sentiment
around the country. The Vietnam War wasn't popular with
the people, nor was the idea of joining the military, but this
was something I'd planned on all my life. To be a pilot and to
fly the supersonic jets, I would have to join the military, but
at least I wouldn't be joining alone. Tom going with me to
training was comforting.

With doubts about my decision, a high school friend, Danny
Fontana, told me to talk to his mother about my decision to
join the military. His mother, Dottie, was like a second mother
to me in high school. She sat down with me and looked
me directly in the eyes and said, "Go after your dream to
become a military jet pilot." Dottie made me feel better about

everything.

Fortunately for me, U.S. military involvement in Vietnam ended on August 15, 1973, and the capture of Saigon by the Vietnam People's Army in April 1975 marked the end of the war. North and South Vietnam were reunified the following year with a Communist government. The death toll for the United States was 58,282 service members killed and more than 300,000 injured; 3,000,000 Vietnamese soldiers and civilians lost their lives. I was just glad this terrible war was finally over.

I was troubled just a couple of months before I joined the military, in June of 1972, when a group of White House operatives broke into the Democratic National Committee's Headquarters at the Watergate Hotel Complex in Washington, D.C. Their task was to spy on the activities and progress of the 1972 Democratic Presidential candidate, Senator George McGovern. The Watergate break-in was a political scandal that continued for two years with the Nixon administration's attempted cover up of its involvement. The fallout of the scandal led to the resignation of Richard Nixon, the only American President to ever resign his office. The scandal also resulted in the indictment, trial, conviction and incarceration of 43 people, including dozens of top Nixon administration officials. Here I was joining military service, and the Commander-in-Chief was a "crook." Man, I felt betrayed.

That summer I felt it was time for me to move out of the house and live on my own. Nick's brother, George, was looking for roommates for his three-bedroom apartment near the campus. I told my dad I was moving out, and he was gracious enough to tell me that if things didn't work out I could move back, but I was determined to make it on my own.

Also that summer, I paid a visit to the Phoenix College football coach, Shanty Hogan, and told him I wanted to try out for the football team. He said I could try out as an offensive center or defensive end. Try outs were at the end of August in the full heat of the summer, but I gave it my all and made the team. This was a whole new level of football. This was not high school sports! The Phoenix metro area's best athletes were on the team preparing for the university level. The competition was fierce. The physical punishment I endured was enormous, but if I was going to be a Marine I needed the mental and physical discipline from college football to get me to that level. I would have a tougher road than I had imagined.

The football season began in September 1972 and I found myself playing sporadically. I was on special team squads, but the offensive center ahead of me made the all-American team the prior year and started all the games. With just two games to go, and during practice running through tires on the ground, my ankle turned and I heard a crack in my left foot. A sharp pain shot through my foot and leg. I hobbled off the practice field but the coaches told me to get back and continue the drills. After practice I had the trainer look at my foot and he told me it was okay. He said it only needed to be taped up. The next day I had my foot taped and went to practice, but the pain got worse. The coaches thought I was just loafing. That evening after practice I went to my family doctor who took x-rays. The doctor discovered three broken bones in my foot, which meant my foot would be in a plaster cast and I'd be leaving the doctor's office on crutches. I was out for the season; my football career was over. The head football coach apologized for the way he treated me during practice, but that was little consolation. Football was something I enjoyed, and it wasn't the only thing I wouldn't be able to do for a few weeks. I couldn't work either, and my military aspirations were in jeopardy.

I was physically disqualified from military training for several months until I finally received a clean bill of health in April 1973, just a few weeks before my summer military training in Quantico. I had to get into shape and fast. My roommate, George, worked with me every day to make it happen. We pumped weights together, and ran long distances and short sprints. My foot was 100% and I was physically and mentally ready for the challenge of officer training. George assured me I was ready for the Marine Corps.

In June of 1973, Tom Keefe and I were on a flight to Quantico for six weeks of hell. My brother, Bob, and his wife, Birda, were in Washington, D.C., touring the Capital on vacation and made it a point to meet me at Washington National Airport when the plane landed. It was nice to see friendly faces, but within a few minutes military personal directed me to a drab green military bus for the 40-minute ride to Marine Corps Base, Quantico, Virginia. The sun was down and it was dark when we pulled up to Camp Upshur on the base. The bus came to a stop and we sat nervously until the Platoon Sergeant walked on the bus and yelled, "GET OFF THE DAMN BUS, YOU BUNCH OF LADIES!!!!" Well, maybe he didn't say ladies, but I can't write exactly what he said!!

"Oh, my God," I thought as we rushed off the bus and lined up next to the squad bay. What was I thinking when I signed up for this life? With all the chaos and yelling we managed to form a single line in front of the barber shop, and one by one we got our heads shaved, just like dad did to me for years. Then off to the medical facility for a number of vaccinations in each arm, then to a large warehouse where we received our military issue of clothing and bedding. We then were rushed into an open squad bay where we were given two minutes to make our racks and get bedded down for the night. It was lights out after that. Only then could I think clearly about what just happened. I lay quietly in my rack with my heart beating rapidly against my chest. Tom was in the bunk to the left of me. I whispered to him, "What the hell did you get me into?"

He replied, "I think we both screwed up big time."

We lay quiet for I don't know how long. We were in the military now, and there was no turning back. Time for sleep!

CHAPTER 18

At 4:30 in the morning, the lights came on in the squad bay and all hell broke loose as the Platoon Sergeant threw an empty garbage can down the aisle of the squad bay. The can crashed down its path between the rows of bunks. My brain snapped to attention and began to function, reminding me where I was as I woke up from a deep sleep. I jumped to my feet as the Platoon Sergeant began what I would come to learn would be his daily rant about how we were all a bunch of #&@#, and we would never make it to the end of training.

"SO YOU WANT TO BE OFFICERS, DO YOU? I DON'T THINK SO!!" he shouted. I stared at the several rows of his Vietnam combat ribbons across the chest of his uniform. Among them were three Silver Stars and four Bronze Stars and numerous campaign ribbons. He had his Smokey the Bear hat on and his eyes were milky white with venom. To me he was Lucifer himself in the flesh. All he needed was a forked tail. With those heroic medals he must have been to hell and back in Vietnam. How could I ever get through this training? This young kid from Arizona was going to be challenged like I had never been challenged before.

The first few days of training were spent getting acclimated to the muggy, hot summer weather of Northern Virginia. We were issued our packs, boots, 782 gear (camping and hiking gear) and the M-14 rifle. The rifle was "never, never, never ever" to be out of my sight if it was not locked up. Tom was assigned to another platoon, so I didn't see much of him during training. I was assigned to Lima Company, 1st Platoon, with Platoon Commander Captain Converse, and Sergeant Instructor Gunny Sergeant Bodnarak, who along with Sergeant Smith conducted our training. By the second week we had mail call, and letters were distributed to us from our loved ones. Their words of encouragement were welcome.

At the time, I was dating a girl named Nancy from Phoenix, who wrote to me almost every day. Along with her letters, and a few from my mom, I was able to stay motivated throughout the training. I became close with my platoon mates. One guy, Mike Anderson, never received a single letter. So I had my sister, Mary Ann, write to him to keep him encouraged to finish training. Mike and Mary Ann would stay friends for a couple years. Later in my military career I ran into Mike and we laughed about those days in Quantico. During our training, however, our time there was no laughing matter, but it did make us stronger in many ways.

After each week of training I became more and more confident that I would do well and finish training. By the fifth week I was marching 10 to 20 miles with a full pack, rifle, helmet and other equipment. The final week of training concluded with a two-day mock war that pitted platoon against platoon. Approximately 70% of the officer candidates successfully completed training, with the others being rejected for different reasons, from mental issues to physical problems. There was also the option to DOR (Drop on Request) for those who found the military life not suited to them. To be an officer, one had to want to be an officer more than anything else.

Of everything I faced during training, I found the mental games that the platoon leaders played with me to be the most difficult. They used several methods to weed the weakest of us from the group, such as long and fatiguing days, but I figured I could handle anything for six weeks and found my way to graduation day with honors.

After graduation we were given airline tickets to return home. My sister, Jean, and her husband, Jonathon, lived in Silver Spring, Maryland, so I delayed my flight a week to spend time with them. They had a little girl named Jennifer. It was great to spend time with her. I spoiled my niece with lots of attention. This visit also gave me a chance to see our nation's capital and its many federal buildings and monuments. I remember being really impressed with their beauty and size. I was proud to be an American! I also took a train to New York City for a day to visit the Big Apple. I toured Time Square and Wall Street, and took a boat ride around the Statue of Liberty. I had a great time and could have stayed forever, but soon I was on my way back to Phoenix.

For the remainder of the summer of 1973, I mowed lawns and worked at the pharmacy. I spent one week camping in the White Mountains of Northern Arizona. My friends, Danny Fontana, Dave Brouchhouser and a St. Gregory's priest, Father Bob Skagen, all went along. It was a blast, and the last fun I would have for a while. We fished at Hawley Lake in the White Mountains. The cool breezes and towering pine trees made a great getaway after my six-week ordeal. We had a small boat with an electric motor that we used to troll around the crystal clear mountain lake and fished for rainbow trout. Life was good. I loved my friends and felt a sense of peace as we all fell asleep at night in the wilderness.

CHAPTER 19

As the summer came to an end, it was time to start Arizona State University for my final two years of college. I relocated to Tempe and moved in with my brother, Steve, who was living near the campus. He had finished ASU the year prior and continued to live there with a good friend of his, Tom Dugal. I rode my motorcycle to and from class, which allowed me to keep gasoline and insurance costs down, especially since tuition had become more expensive. I kept my lawn service and mowed lawns on weekends to help pay the rent and tuition. A long-distance romance was too difficult to maintain, so Nancy and I broke up. Plus, I had to focus more on my studies. In order to get my military commission I needed good grades. I took on another job cleaning swimming pools for some extra money. I was barely keeping my head above water financially, but I met all my fiscal commitments just barely.

In October, the members of the Organization of Arab Petroleum Exporting Countries or the OAPEC proclaimed an oil embargo. This was in response to the U.S. decision to re-supply the Israeli military during the Yom Kippur War. It lasted until March of the following year and sent gasoline prices skyrocketing fourfold. I remember how grateful I was to only have a motorcycle tank to fill as I waited in long lines.

I was fortunate to be able to pass those lines most days; they formed each day at gas stations to buy gasoline early in the morning. However, my motorcycle didn't save me entirely, because the price of gas shot up just as I began private flying lessons to help prepare me for military flight school. Timing is everything.

In January of 1974 I started attending Sawyer Aviation at Phoenix Sky Harbor Airport for flight training. Although prices were up for gas, I had saved enough money over the Christmas break to start flight ground school, and in February took my first flight lesson. I wanted every possible edge to make it to jet training. With private flight lessons I figured I'd be a jump ahead of others wanting to get to the jet pipeline in military flight school.

On February 11, 1974, my flight instructor, Richard Glazar, and I took to the skies over Phoenix in a Cessna 150, a small two-seat, single propeller engine, high-wing airplane. I recall as we lifted off the runway that this was my destiny… to become a pilot. I looked down as the city of Phoenix got smaller and smaller. I felt a sense of calm wash over me. After about a month of training, one day we landed at Scottsdale airport and Rich told me to park the airplane. He said to let him out so I could do a few solo landings. My heart swelled. I was ready! I took the end of the runway and off I went without an instructor by my side on my first solo flight. That was on March 12.

Just a few months later, May 31, 1974, I passed my flight test and was awarded my private pilot's license by Darrell Sawyer himself. The very next day I took my dad flying over Roosevelt Lake, a large body of water northeast of Phoenix, and we had a great time. My dad and I traded off taking the controls, and for almost an hour and a half it was just him and me having the time of our lives. My dad hadn't flown after the war because of the cost of renting an airplane, so he soaked it all in as we maneuvered the Cessna 150 with steep turns and low-level flying. I will never forget my dad's face as he took the controls. He was in Heaven, and so was I! It was a fantastic experience for us both.

With my third year of college complete, it was once again time to head back to Quantico for my final six-week training session. I was in great physical shape and ready to get the training completed. I was less than a year away from earning my Second Lieutenant commission. Tom dropped out of the program, but I was super motivated to get back to training. Off I went back to Quantico to face the same harassment I faced the first night a year earlier. It was the same with the drill of getting off the bus, the haircut and all the yelling. Only I had changed. I asked myself why I wanted to be back at this place again? The answer was because I really wanted to reach my goal of becoming a pilot, but my dreams were almost dashed.

Late that night when we were getting our physical exams and vaccines I was pulled aside by a nurse and sent to a private room. A doctor came in and took my blood pressure again and told me it was too high to go into training. I thought, "Of course it is high after being up for over 30 hours and paraded around like cattle." Was this the end of my dream? Was I going to be sent home and discharged? Was my blood pressure really that high? I'm a young guy is all I could think. This could not be!!

The next day everyone started training except me. I was told I would have my blood pressure taken three times a day for two days to see if would show normal levels. If not, my military career would be over before it began. Luck was with me. After the two days, I was cleared for training and assigned to 3rd Platoon, F Company, for the duration of the six weeks of training. It was the same routine as the prior summer, so I just had to gut it out and finish. After the third week we were given Sundays off and we each received liberty passes to leave the base. Some of us got a hotel just off base to relax in a soft bed and get away from everything. It was good to get a good night's sleep away from all the harassment. I needed all the rest I could get; and I was about to fall for the wrong gal…

CHAPTER 20

One afternoon during the fourth week of training I was in the mess hall making my way through the chow line for lunch when a civilian employee who was serving potatoes passed me a note under my tray. She was a young college student with a summer job at the base serving the troops. I slid the note into my pocket and waited till I had a chance to read it in private. When I got to my bunk later that night and carefully unfolded the note, I was thrilled. This pretty girl had given me her name and phone number. Her note said I should call her for a date for the following Sunday. She knew we had Sundays off. This is unreal! My mind raced. In the middle of training I was going to have a date, but wait a minute. Was this a trick or something? I shared the note with my platoon buddies and they were in disbelief. We had all been fantasizing about this young woman during our first three weeks in training and now it looked as if I may have a date with her. I was on Cloud Nine. My bunkmates were full of envy.

The following Saturday night, with my buddies keeping guard, I slipped out of the barracks to a pay phone near the Captain's office. I could see him through the window talking with other instructors. I put a dime in the slot on the phone and cringed as it jingled down into the guts of the machine hoping the Captain didn't hear it. Hands a little sweaty, I dialed the girl's number. I was breathing so heavily that I was sure the Captain would hear me and come outside to jump down my throat.

After a couple of rings a man answered and said, "This is Chief Warrant Officer Anti."

Oh, my God, now what do I do? I took a deep breath and meekly said, "This is Officer Candidate Raths and I would like to speak to Sharon, please."

After a long pause, the man replied, "Hang on. Let me get her."

Sharon came to the phone after what seemed to be several minutes. "Are you the candidate I slipped the note to?" Her voice sounded lyrical and sweet. I almost couldn't answer.

"Yes, yes. My name is Greg," I replied. Our conversation went along more easily from there. She told me that her father was an active duty Marine Corps Chief Warrant Officer stationed at Quantico, and she was a college sophomore at The University of Massachusetts, and was home for the summer living with her parents on base. I told her a few things about me and we made a date for the next day, and I hung up. In the darkness I quietly slipped back into the barracks and told the guys that she was going to pick me up in the morning for a picnic to the Shenandoah National Park along the Blue Ridge Mountains in Virginia. They all howled like a bunch of coyotes. This was crazy; I could hardly sleep that night.

The next morning Sharon came to the barracks in her parents' car and picked me up, but before we headed for the picnic, she told me her parents wanted to meet me. She drove to her house and I followed her inside. Her mother and father were waiting for us. I extended my hand. Sharon's father, a tall stoic man, met it with a firm grasp that said it all. I wasn't to take advantage of his daughter.

Sharon's mother was gracious and asked a lot of questions. I must have passed muster, because I finally received her parents' blessing to spend the day with their daughter. Whew! Off we went to the mountains, talking and laughing all the way. We hiked down some trails and before we knew it, we had to head back to the base. I had to be back to the barracks by 2000 hours, that is 8:00 p.m., and her parents had invited me for dinner at 6:00 p.m., so I didn't want to be late for either. As we drove back onto the base, the Marine sentry at the front gate snapped to and gave us a salute. That was a greeting only for officers, but quickly realizing our car had an officer's base sticker on the windshield, I gave him back a snappy salute. Dang, that felt good. Yes, I really want to be an officer in the Marines, I thought.

Once we got back to the Anti house, just as in youth, I couldn't turn down a turkey dinner. I knew I was in when Sharon's dad wished me the best in my training. After dinner her parents had to leave to go to a military function. Sharon and I had just under an hour to spend together in the comfort of her home. We made another date for the following Sunday. Sharon dropped me off at the barracks just before curfew. She gave me a kiss good night and I was hooked. When I entered the barracks my buddies began asking for details.

"No details. Just let's say it went great!" I said, all smiles.

Getting to know Sharon made training a lot more fun. I couldn't wait for lunch every day to see her because she would slip me chocolate bars and suggestive notes while giving me her cutest smile and a wink. After week five, she picked me up for a fun-filled Sunday in Washington, D.C. We went to Arlington National Cemetery, the Marine Corps Memorial and a few other sites. We had lunch in Alexandria and headed to her house for another home-cooked dinner. Things just couldn't get any better, I thought, but when she dropped me off she mentioned that my Platoon Sergeant had been asking her out, too. She said that she had refused his advances and told him that she was dating one of his officer candidates. She further told him that she didn't want to date him.

"You told him what?" I exclaimed. This can't be happening, I thought. "Did you tell him my name?"

"No, no. Of course not. I would never do that," she said, looking down. I admit that I didn't believe her. No matter. We would soon find out.

I was a little uneasy with the situation when I returned to the barracks that night. Just before lights out, the Platoon Sergeant came into the barracks. We all jumped to attention at the foot of our beds. Here's where it got a little weird.

He shouted, "ROMEO, ROMEO, WHEREFORE ART THOU, ROMEO?"

My heart pounded. Did he know it was me who was dating Sharon?

He continued. "No one is going to bed tonight until I find out which one of you is taking out the mess hall honey!" he bellowed.

I could feel the eyes of my buddies turn to me in betrayal. Slowly the Platoon Sergeant walked down the aisle and stopped only when he was standing right in front of me. He then blared, "YOU HAVE 10 SECONDS TO IDENTIFY YOURSELF OR WE ARE ALL GOING ON A 20-MILE FORCED NIGHT MARCH."

At that point I stepped forward and said with as steady a voice I could force through my lips, "I am the officer candidate who has been going out with the mess hall honey, Sir."

He told me to meet him outside and as he followed me out he turned off the lights. The guys went back to bed. My heart raced, but I knew I hadn't broken any rules. I only took Sharon out when I had a liberty pass, and I made it back to the barracks before curfew.

Outside I was standing tall in front of the Sergeant when he told me to relax. He said, "I know you didn't do anything wrong, but I want to date Sharon, and I want you to tell her to go out with me on a date."

What was happening? How could I do that, feeling like I did about Sharon? I found myself in a real jam because I knew Sharon would never agree to go out with him, nor did I want him anywhere near her. He took me to his office and told me to call her and make the date for him. My mind was going a million miles a minute trying to figure out a way out of this predicament. I slowly dialed her number, digit by digit, as I watched the rotary dial stop after each number. When I got through to Sharon she was surprised that I was calling her so late after curfew, but she understood when I explained the whole situation to her while the Sergeant watched me closely and listened to every word. Luckily for me, Sharon picked up on what was going on and told me to tell the Sergeant she would be happy to go out with him next Sunday, the day after I left for home. She told me to put him on the phone and said she was looking forward for their date on Sunday. The Sergeant appeared satisfied and sent me back to the barracks. Monday at lunch Sharon slipped me a message telling me she never intended to be available for the date and she knew I would be gone and he couldn't do anything about it. Clever girl.

On Friday I graduated, and on Saturday morning I boarded

the bus headed to the airport. I was going home. Sharon canceled the date as my bus exited the base. I smiled all the way home, looking down from my little airplane window at the clouds that passed below, thinking of Sharon. I kept in touch with her for a while, but once we both went back to college the relationship ended. I will never forget the summer of 1974.

CHAPTER 21

When I got back to Phoenix I used some of the pay I received during training to do some flying. I checked out in a Cessna 172, a four-seat, more powerful version of the Cessna 150, and took my friends flying. I asked Jimmy O'Connor, who was dating his future wife, Kathy Morris, at the time, to go flying with me. I took a friend and the four of us would have a double-dating air adventure.

Jimmy was hesitant at first because he was afraid he might get air sick, but after Kathy challenged his manhood, he agreed. I rented a plane out of the Glendale airport and off we went. Jim and I sat in the front seat at the controls; Kathy and my friend rode in the back seat. Jim was having the time of his life. We flew up north around Lake Pleasant and buzzed some of the boaters who were pulling skiers. The air was smooth and we were having a great time. Kathy was feeling miserable in the back and used her airsick bag more than once. Ironic, I thought.

During my senior year at ASU, I expanded my lawn service that included keeping the grounds of Bourgade High School groomed. I needed more money for rent, tuition and flying, so I walked into the office of the principal of Bourgade and told him that if he wanted more students to be attracted to his high school, he needed the grounds to be groomed properly. I asked him to give me one day before making a decision to hire me. The next day I mowed and trimmed the front lawn of the school and trimmed all the palm trees. The principal, Father Waldren, was so impressed with my work that he hired me on the spot. I then hired Jim to help me. We had our work cut out for us since we were both in college and neither of us had a lot of spare time. Fortunately for me, my brother Ron went up to Alaska with some of his friends to work on the trans-Alaskan oil pipeline and left me his pickup truck. Jim and I became very close friends that year. We groomed all the athletic fields and kept the campus looking sharp.

A week before the 1974 Fiesta Bowl at Sun Devil Stadium in Tempe, the organizing committee sponsored a 26-mile marathon for December 21, 1974. Just a few months before I was to receive my officer commission I thought it was best for me to get into top physical shape, so I signed up for the marathon and began to prepare for the run.

On a cool winter morning near Saguaro Lake about 300 runners lined up to start the run. The race would take us runners on a small blacktop road through the desert. Each side of the road was adorned with large saguaro cactus, yucca plants, bright red rocks and jagged hills. My cousin, Jim Jorgensen, 15 years old at the time, rode his bike alongside me to give me water and keep me motivated. I did well as I ran on the hilly road until the 18-mile mark when I hit the wall and felt totally fatigued. I broke stride and started walking. Jim did his best to encourage me to get back into a stride, and after about a mile of walking, I regained my strength, finishing the race just over four hours. Feeling a sense of accomplishment, but totally exhausted, I lay on the ground just past the finish line as my cousin poured water on my face. This would be my first and last marathon. The following week I went to the Fiesta Bowl and watched Oklahoma State defeat Brigham Young University 16-6.

On New Year's Eve, Jim O'Connor's dad hosted a huge party at St. Vincent DePaul's Catholic Church social hall. Before the party we all watched the amazing Sugar Bowl where the Nebraska Cornhuskers came from behind to beat the Florida Gators 13-10. Jim brought Kathy, and I took Jim's sister, Jeannie. We all had a great time and ushered in 1975 with midnight hugs and kisses. I knew it would be a good year. The Vietnam War had ended, the Watergate scandal was over, President Ford was bringing the country back from "that long national nightmare" and I was to graduate in May from ASU with a Bachelor of Science degree, and I would receive my Officer commission. There was a lot to celebrate and to be thankful for.

After the dance we all went to Jimmy's house and played poker. Jim's dad and his friends were at one table – called the "big boys' table" – and Jimmy and I were at our own table playing with much smaller stakes with our friends. As the night went on, our table's game was over, so I moved to an empty seat at the big boys' table. I had a few dollars to gamble and they were burning a hole in my pocket. I had $20, which in my terms meant four lawn jobs. Slowly my stack of chips dwindled to just a few dollars when Mr. O'Connor loaned me $80 to keep me in the game. By 4:00 the next morning my chips were all gone and I was out $100. That was a huge loss for me to handle with my tight budget, but it was also another good lesson for me. I took on extra work during my winter break and sold my motorcycle to pay Mr. O'Connor back.

During my final semester of college I had to take only four classes to graduate. This gave me more time to work. My brother was still in Alaska, so I could still use his truck. Jimmy and I continued to work the Bourgade grounds and we took on other jobs. With my departure for the Marines just a few months away, Jim asked to take over my lawn service. Fine by me; it's all yours, Jimmy.

That spring I turned most of the operations over to Jim. In February, the head baseball coach at Bourgade asked if I would be interested in coaching the Junior Varsity team that spring. I accepted and thoroughly enjoyed coaching, finishing the season 8-7. After the baseball season, Father Waldron called me into his office and offered me a full-time teaching and coaching job. He also offered me a vacant room at the rectory to live in at no cost. I was now conflicted. Do I stay in

Phoenix with all my friends or do I pursue my aviation career in the military? I pondered my dilemma. Military service was my choice hands down.

My report date would be July 7, 1975, to The Basic School at Quantico, Virginia. This would be a six-month school where I would learn the basics of Marine Corps infantry and other occupational skills the Marine Corps offered. After completion of The Basic School, I had orders to the Naval Air Station in Pensacola, Florida, for flight school.

With graduation over at ASU in early May 1975, I had a few weeks to gather my belongings and prepare for the drive to Virginia. The military sent me a letter to report to Luke Air Force Base for my final physical exam before reporting. With the high blood pressure issue still in my head from summer training I was nervous as I watched the Air Force nurse place the blood pressure cuff around my arm and pumped air into it. She slowly let the air out and read my blood pressure. The look in her eyes said it all. I knew she was going to tell me that it was high. She took my readings two more times, but each time my blood pressure climbed. I couldn't believe what was happening. My whole future was crumbling in front of my eyes… again. I told her I was nervous and she told me to sit a while and she would take it again, but each time it was high. I left the base clinic almost in tears.

I received a letter from the military to report to the nearest medical facility and have my blood pressure recorded for two weeks, twice a day. I went to the ASU health center with the letter and a kind nurse told me just to relax as long as I wanted before she did my blood pressure test. Throughout the two weeks my blood pressure was normal and the military gave me the go ahead from my commissioning. To say I was relieved doesn't come close to what I felt.

CHAPTER 22

On May 24, 1975, my friends and family gathered at brother Bob's house for my commissioning ceremony. Captain Guerin from the Officer Selection Office in Phoenix came to do the honors of swearing me in. I wore my dress white uniform and my parents had the honor to pin my Second Lieutenant gold bars on my shoulder epaulettes.

With family and friends to witness this monumental event in my life, I took the following oath as I raised my right hand and repeated, "I, Gregory G. Raths, do solemnly swear that I will support and defend the Constitution of the United States against all enemies, foreign and domestic; that I will bear true faith and allegiance to the same; that I take this obligation freely, without any mental reservation or purpose of evasion; and that I will well and faithfully discharge the office upon which I am about to enter. So help me God."

It was official. I was now a commissioned officer in the United States Marine Corps. This was the proudest day of my life to this point. My parents were proud. My mother cried.

Jim O'Connor threw me a farewell party at his parents' house a week before I left Phoenix that lasted all night. I packed up my belongings and threw them into the back of brother's pickup truck to leave Phoenix after nearly 21 years of living there. This was not an easy thing to do, but I felt it was my destiny to become a military jet pilot. Two days before I was to leave for Virginia my mother asked me if she and my youngest brother Danny, then age 10, could go along on the trip. She said they would fly back once I arrived in Quantico. Being flat broke at the time, with just enough money for gas, I thought it would be a good idea, so on July 1, 1975, off we went. We camped along the way at KOAs (Kampgrounds of America) in a small tent we had brought with us. We had a great time traveling across the country, stopping in New Mexico, Texas, Louisiana and Tennessee. In New Orleans, the truck broke down with an oil pump problem, but that only set us back a day. When we hit Knoxville, Tennessee, my mom and brother were ready to get home, so I dropped them off at the Knoxville Airport. I would finish the trip on my own. The following evening, I reported to The Basic School in Quantico, and I was now on Uncle Sam's payroll. I had only $30 in my pocket, but I had made it.

Assigned to Alpha Company, 4th Platoon, I began the basic officer course. Each platoon had about 40 Second Lieutenants led by a seasoned Captain. The Company was commanded by a Major. The first two weeks included classes and fittings for uniforms. Officers must buy their own uniforms with the total cost at around $1,000 for all the dress uniforms and their accessories, plus the everyday uniforms. The uniform shop on base gave me credit and provided a payment plan, so here

I was two weeks on active duty and already a grand in debt. Nevertheless, I enjoyed the training and meeting new friends. I shared a room with Dave Rann, who also wanted to be an aviator, so we had a lot to talk about throughout training. Dave graduated from The Citadel, a military prep college in Charleston, South Carolina, and his father was an active duty Colonel in the Marine Corps. Dave knew the nitty-gritty of military life, and he was a great help to me when it came to military procedure and protocol.

On November 10, 1975, we celebrated the 200th birthday of the Marine Corps with a birthday ball in our school's ballroom. I needed to find a date for the ball so I went with a couple buddies to the all-girls college, Mary Washington College in Fredericksburg, Virginia, one Saturday night. We sort of crashed a sorority party where we mingled a bit. Before the night ended it was mission accomplished. On the night of the ball I picked up my date, a southern belle beauty, at her sorority house on campus. I wore my dress blue uniform and she wore a long formal dress. She was like an angel in an aqua dress! Just like in the movies, she walked down a wide formal carpeted staircase to the reception area at her high society sorority house where I was eagerly awaiting. She blushed just a little as I presented her with a white rose corsage. A week before I bought a 1974 Chevrolet Malibu. I now proudly walked my date to the car. Finally, at age 21, I owned my first car. Of course, I didn't mention this to my date. She had no idea that she could be riding in a beat up pick-up truck! The ball would be my last opportunity for a while to kick up my heels, so we danced a lot and had a great time. After that it was business as usual.

At Christmas we were given two weeks off for the holidays. Since my brother would be returning soon from Alaska, I had to get his truck back to him, so I drove it home for Christmas. After four days on the road I pulled up at Bob's house. It was a sight to behold, all lit up with Christmas lights. He was hosting a Christmas Eve party, and as I walked up the sidewalk I could see everyone laughing and carrying on in the front room. I was so excited to be home that I couldn't wait to get inside. I opened up the front door and shouted, "I'm here."

Until that moment I don't think I realized just how much I had missed everyone. Everyone I cared about was there, my parents, siblings, my Aunt Rita and Uncle Bob and my three cousins. It was like in the movie It's a Wonderful Life when George Bailey was warmly welcomed home by his family on Christmas Eve in Bedford Falls. I received hugs and kisses from everyone and we broke into song, I'll Be Home for Christmas. We sang Christmas carols and then later went to midnight Mass at St. Gregory's Church. I was filled with pride sitting in the pew wearing my Marine Corps dress blue uniform. It was great to be home among family and friends. I didn't want to go back to Virginia, but I had to all too soon.

I flew back to Quantico to finish the final few weeks of training. Our graduation was scheduled for January 26, 1976, and we all anticipated our transfer to our next duty station. Most of us lieutenants who had received aviation contracts were ready to head south to the warm white sandy beaches of Pensacola Beach. One last hurdle before graduation was to qualify at the rifle range with the M-16 automatic assault rifle. Throughout the training I had competed fairly well, but now it was time to earn my rifle badge, a badge that I could wear on my uniform. After two days of shooting at various yard lines in the dead of winter in Virginia, I qualified as Rifle Expert, earning the highest score in the platoon. No one can ever say I was an underachiever! This badge was important to me and I worked hard to get it. Next, all I wanted was those Navy Wings displayed prominently above my left shirt pocket, but that would come after a long road ahead.

After graduation, I packed up my Malibu and drove down to Florida for flight training. Pensacola was my idea of heaven with plenty of warm sunshine and deep blue skies. Man, was this ever different from Phoenix and Virginia! The gulf was warm and crystal clear, and it sparkled as the sunrays glistened off the water. I loved standing on the beach watching the waves lick the bright white sand. I never tired of the beauty.

As I drove onto the Naval Air Station, a sign displayed the phrase, "Welcome to the Cradle of Naval Aviation." As I watched the jets flying above me I longed to begin flight school. I was ready! With 80% of Marine Corps flight students selected for helicopters after primary flight training, I had to give it my all to get a slice of that 20% quota for jets. I vowed then and there that I would be a jet pilot, even if I had to study 20 hours a day.

CHAPTER 23

Flight school began with six weeks of ground school, which included classes in aerodynamics, physics, mathematics, jet engine propulsion, meteorology, aviation physiology and physical fitness. The first week of training included a variety of tests, to include: color blindness and night vision awareness training, centrifuge G-force training, obstacle course fitness workouts, swimming qualification, and eye and ear exams. And then I was given another full physical examination with all the blood work and probing, and most important, blood pressure normal. After that, every inch of my body was measured, from my neck size, seated height, standing height and length of my arms. At first it seemed odd with all the measuring, but then I wondered if my being 6' 3" made me too tall for jets? Would my measurements keep me from a jet cockpit? My height came in just under the wire and I proceeded to the next phase of training.

After I made it through the initial tests and exams, the senior Marine Officer, Colonel Shaffer, came into our classroom and gave us the standard welcome aboard speech. "Look around this classroom," he said loudly, looking at each of us squarely in the eyes. "Most of you will never get through this training." With that, he shut up to let his comment sink in. Then he continued with a brief unmemorable speech.

Wow. With such a huge vote of confidence from that man I was more determined than ever before to get over each and every hurdle. On the last day of ground school with all the academic exams complete, I was cleared for flight training and began the yearlong journey to get my Naval Aviator Wings. The next day I received my flight equipment: flight suits, helmet, gloves, kneeboard, flight boots, sunglasses and the coveted leather flight jacket. That was one of the things I wanted most!

I was transferred for primary flight training to Naval Air Station Saufley Field, Florida, a small outlying airfield about 10 miles north of Pensacola. I was assigned to my first military squadron, Navy Training Squadron 1 (VT-1), where I flew the T-34B Mentor, a propeller-driven, single-engine military trainer. My grades from ground school would be combined with my primary flight training grades to determine if I would fly helicopters or jets. C'mon jets!!

I was assigned my flight instructor, Navy Lt. Paul Johnson, an S-2F Tracker fleet pilot, who was now training new pilots in the T-34B. After a few flight simulator training sessions and a couple of exams on flight procedures and orientation of the local area flight rules, I was ready for my first flight. I couldn't be more excited. I wanted to shout from the rooftops that I was going to make it and nobody was going to stop me.

On April 29, 1976, with my flight instructor in the back seat

I took runway 05 at Saufley Field, revved up the engine and started my roll down the 4,000-foot runway. After several hundred feet, the nose got light as I pulled back on the stick. The aircraft took to the air for my first flight in a military aircraft. I flew around the training area, looking for the landmarks to keep me in the area, and then started my training with steep turns, stall recoveries and slow flight. My instructor would demonstrate a maneuver and then I would attempt it. After about an hour of training we headed back to Saufley Field for some touch-and-go landing practice. My first flight of the required 20 for primary training was now under my belt, and it felt good to be in the air. That was the first thing to celebrate. The second is that my military flight pay kicked in that day, giving me a couple extra hundred dollars a month. I was flying high!

The flight maneuvers on each flight were graded average, above average or below average. I had to net at least one or two above average scores per flight to help ensure I would get assigned to jets. As I was completing training my grades were looking good compared to the other Marines in my class. I was sitting in the top two when it came to my final check flight. I was assigned the Commander of the Air Wing, Navy Captain Twigger, who was known to be a tough grader and a "screamer." A few flight instructors got that nickname for their high volume critique of a maneuver over the intercom. With all the pressure on my shoulders for this final check flight, it did not go as well as I hoped. I messed up on a couple of maneuvers and knew when I parked the aircraft that my dream of flying jets was in jeopardy.

After receiving my flight debrief, the Captain gave me two net below averages, shattering any hope for jet training. Fortunately, on June 3, 1976, the senior Marine officer at the flight school brought me into his office and told me I was one of the two Marine flight students that would be assigned jets. Holy cow… I made it!

The other Marine was my good friend, Steve Smyser. We were given the choice to go to Texas or Mississippi for jet flight training, and since I had been dating a girl from Gulf Breeze, Florida, I took Mississippi. That would put me closer to her for weekend visits. That afternoon I sent my dad a three-word telegram: "I GOT JETS." I wish I could have been there to see his face. I knew he was proud. Later I would learn that he told all of his friends at work and in the neighborhood. I could just see him at the bar of the Yo Yo Tavern buying his friends drinks to celebrate.

CHAPTER 24

In June of 1976, I flew home to Phoenix for my brother Steve's wedding. He married a girl he had been dating for a couple years, Cecile. This gave me the opportunity to be with family and friends, not only to celebrate my brother's wedding, but also to celebrate my getting to fly jets.

In early July, my buddy, Steve, and I received our orders to Naval Air Station Meridian, Mississippi, and were assigned to Navy Training Squadron 19 (VT-19). The air base is about 15 miles north of the city of Meridian. The base was built in 1961 in the middle of nowhere. Senior Mississippi Senator John Stennis sponsored legislation to appropriate funds for the base to help Mississippi's economy. The airfield operations area was named McCain Field in honor of the late Admiral John S. McCain, Sr., of Teoc, Mississippi. It was a beautiful base. Steve and I, along with several Navy flight students, began an intense ground school and basic jet simulator training. I moved into the bachelor officer's quarters on base where I found myself studying late every night. Needless to say, I was too busy to maintain my relationship with the girl for whom I had chosen Mississippi. Besides, she found a Navy pilot in Pensacola to date and later marry. Her loss!!

On July 28, 1976, I flew my first flight in a military jet aircraft, the T-2C Buckeye. With my instructor, Navy Lt. Klint, in the back seat, we took to the skies over Mississippi. What a thrilling experience! The T-2C is a straight-wing trainer with two jet engines. I could feel the power come up through my body as the two jet engines wound up to full speed during the take-off roll. Once in the air I did loops, wingovers and other maneuvers that made me want to yell out loud. I had made it to the jet aircraft and was on my way to getting my wings! I would fly the T-2C for about six months in basic jet and then move on to advanced jet training for six more months. My life was moving forward according to my plan. In fact, I couldn't have planned things better.

During that time, my cousin, Jim Jorgensen, was playing his final year of high school football at Alhambra High School in Phoenix. His sister, Marie, was the head cheerleader for the squad. I always wanted to see Jim play and Marie cheer, so on a three-day weekend I flew to Phoenix and surprised them as I waved from the bleachers. They won the game. After that, we hung out at my Aunt Rita's house for a party. Their younger sister, Peggy, joined in the fun, as did some of my friends. Having their support as I progressed in my flight training meant the world to me.

In January 1977, I started advanced jet training in the TA-4J Skyhawk, a single jet engine, swept-wing, Navy trainer. With its swept wings the aircraft was more maneuverable than the

T2-C. I was attached to Navy Training Squadron 7 (VT-7). The training went into more advanced maneuvers, such as air-to-air combat maneuvering, night flying, air-to-ground bombing, aerial gunnery and aircraft carrier qualifications. The course also included cross-country flying. One of my cross-country flights took me to Williams Air Force Base, in Mesa, Arizona, where my family, cousins and friends came out to see me fly in. God, I felt proud as I stepped out of my jet. I don't think my chest could have been more pumped up! I had lunch with everyone before I had to leave to continue my cross-country flight.

Near the end of training, in May of that year, I completed six day carrier landings on the USS Lexington (CV-16) that was steaming in the Gulf of Mexico. This was the most challenging event for me yet, also one of the most rewarding. I recall looking down from my jet at the carrier thinking, "I have to land on that little thing down there!!" I was very anxious as I set up for landing on the ship, but mission successful as I completed the six landings. My training was now over and on June 24 my dad flew out to Meridian to pin my wings on my uniform during a military ceremony at the Officer's Club on base. Six of us from my original class of 40 made it to that special day when we received our Navy gold wings. It was such a good feeling to have my dad there to do the honors. After the winging ceremony I had to wait a couple of weeks to get my fleet aircraft assignment.

My pal Steve received orders to fly the A-6E Intruder in Cherry Point, North Carolina, and my assignment was to fly the RF-4B Phantom II in El Toro, California. I was excited to be heading to southern California, land of beautiful beaches and equally beautiful babes! It was a young man's dream come true.

A Navy buddy of mine, Paul Garvey, got his first choice and went to Jacksonville, Florida, to fly the A-7E Corsair, and another Navy friend, Jim Patterson, got his choice, the F-14 Tomcat at NAS Oceana, Virginia. I was excited for them, but for me it was southern California, here I come!!

CHAPTER 25

Before I could enter the Fleet Marine Force at El Toro and fly
the RF-4B, I had to complete a six-month course at Marine
Corps Air Station, Yuma, Arizona, where I would learn to fly
the F-4 Phantom II. This was one beast of a jet aircraft. The
McDonnell Douglas F-4 Phantom II is a tandem two-seat
(pilot and radar interceptor officer), twin-engine, long-range
supersonic jet interceptor fighter/fighter-bomber. This jet first
entered service in 1960 with the U.S. Navy. Proving highly
adaptable, it was also adopted by the Marine Corps and Air
Force in the mid-1960s. It is a fighter with a top speed of over
Mach 2.1. And I was going to fly her! She was my babe!!!

After two months of ground school and flight simulators,
I strapped into the cockpit of this hog and took off from
MCAS Yuma. As I pushed both engines into full afterburner,
providing over 18,000 pounds of thrust per engine, the aircraft
rumbled under me as I streaked into the skies after a long roll
on runway 03R. The pure power of this jet was unbelievable.
Within a few seconds I was at speeds of over 400 mph as I
passed through 15,000 feet of altitude. What an incredible
aircraft was all I could think. I was just 23 years old and Uncle
Sam gave me this multi-million dollar jet aircraft to take out
for a flight on a warm spring afternoon in Arizona. Life didn't

get any better than this.

Passing 25,000 feet and still accelerating I recalled Gillespie Magee's words from his poem, High Flight...

Up, up the long delirious, burning blue,

I've topped the windswept heights with easy grace

Where never lark or even eagle flew –

And, while with silent lifting mind I've trod

The high untresspassed sanctity of space,

Put out my hand and touched the face of God.

Gillespie sure knew what he was talking about, and now I did, too.

Training at Yuma progressed really well, and since I was so close to Phoenix I could go home on weekends to see family and friends. One weekend I drove to Las Vegas and met Nick and Lori there for a weekend of gambling, partying and dancing.

Back on base, I was having a great time, proudly walking around in my flight suit with my gold wings. I just couldn't wait for my next flight. I was a young man full of bravado. It was hard to contain how I felt. Each flight I learned more and more about the F-4 and its capabilities. I learned to refuel in the air off a KC-130 military tanker, and then after breaking away from the tanker, I would accelerate to supersonic speed. After six months, my training was complete and I received my orders to MCAS El Toro, California.

A buddy of mine, John Nunn, who was already stationed at El Toro, needed a roommate at his apartment in Newport Beach. I jumped at the opportunity. From my window I could see the Pacific Ocean and smell the ocean breeze. Now this was living!

In March 1978, I drove onto the Marine Air Base in El Toro and checked into the Third Marine Aircraft Wing (3rd MAW), and then to Marine Aircraft Group 11 (MAG-11), where I received orders to my first fleet squadron, Marine Tactical Reconnaissance Squadron 3 (VMFP-3). This squadron flew the reconnaissance version of the F-4, also called the RF-4B. The aircraft had several cameras mounted inside the nose to take tactical pictures for the ground forces on the battlefield. It also had an infrared reconnaissance system for nighttime surveillance of a combat zone, too. It was a heck of a great machine.

My Commanding Officer was LtCol Mackey. He welcomed me aboard and assigned me a collateral duty to work for the aircraft maintenance officer, Major O.J. Riddell. I was to supervise the ejection seat and the flight equipment shops. In May, I deployed with a four-plane detachment to MCAS Cherry Point, North Carolina, to participate in a large-scale east coast military exercise, Operation Solid Shield. The exercise lasted for two weeks and I learned a great deal about combined arms exercises. I flew every day with large strike packages comprised of different types of aircraft in the strike group. I was really getting to know my aircraft, as well as the other aircraft in the Marine Corps and Navy inventory. I was learning that time in the cockpit was invaluable to gaining experience. If and when my skills were needed in combat, I wanted to be the best. I could be counted on to perform my mission with expertise.

In September, I flew with a four-plane detachment to Denmark to participate in a three-week NATO exercise. This was my first transoceanic flight in the Phantom II, which included several aerial refueling points across the Atlantic Ocean. As a young, relatively inexperienced aviator, this was a real test for me, but after 11 hours of flying, passing just south of Greenland and Iceland, I saw the coast of Europe and landed at a Danish airfield in Vandel. Several squadrons of NATO aircraft were there to participate in this exercise, Operation Northern Wedding. This was a NATO Cold War military exercise conducted every four years. It was designed to test NATO's ability to rearm and resupply Europe during times of war. The entire experience went well and my friend Steve from flight school was there flying the A-6E.

We managed to get off the base to eat, drink at the local pubs and take in the Danish scenery. The countryside was very green with small farms scattered through the rolling hills. Goats and sheep grazed along the road for a meal of tall, wet grass. One weekend, Steve and I drove into Germany for a day of sightseeing and shopping. I found a beautiful piece of art, a copy of a painting of a mother and her young daughter, which I purchased. I had to laugh when I got home, on the back of the artwork in small print was, "Made in San Francisco." So much for my eye for art, but for a guy from Phoenix this was mighty exciting stuff. I couldn't get enough of it. I was seeing the world. Hmm… I recall my recruiter telling me that I would see the world, and he was right!

When I returned stateside my squadron was assigned a new Commanding Officer in October, LtCol Larry Reiman, and he came to the squadron with unbridled enthusiasm. On one of his first flights with the squadron he scheduled me to fly as his wingman on a training mission. The flight went really well, and on the way back to El Toro he told me to take the lead and bring us back home. I moved out in front to take the lead, and he flew on my wing. As we got closer to the base I started pilot-induced oscillations (PIOs), this occurs when a pilot inadvertently commands an often-increasing series of corrections in opposite directions, each an attempt to cover the aircraft's reaction to the previous input. An aircraft in such a condition can appear to be "porpoising," switching between upward and downward directions. My CO was trying to stay in position on my wing, but then asked me over the radio, "What's going on? Do you have snakes in your cockpit?" Funny, I thought. Just what I need… a comic. I soon settled down and smoothed out. We landed safely. During the debriefing in the squadron's Ready Room, Reiman gave me my call sign, a nickname we use among us pilots. It would be "Snake." That call sign stuck with me for the rest of my military flying career.

In March 1979, I was ordered to the Marine Corps Air Station in Iwakuni, Japan, for a six-month aircraft carrier deployment. Our squadron had four aircraft on the USS Midway (CV-41) based in Yokosuka, Japan, which provided the carrier with tactical reconnaissance support. Before I could transfer to Japan I had to carrier qualify in the Phantom, both day and night, on the west coast aircraft carrier, USS Enterprise (CVN-65). I had to successfully complete 10 day landings and six night landings at sea. I have to admit that I was nervous; I mean real nervous! I had heard horror stories about night carrier landings, and now I was going to be put to the test. Even my dad said he never would want to perform such a difficult feat.

After five weeks of carrier landing practice at El Toro, I took off for the USS Enterprise that was sailing off the coast of San Diego. The day landings went really well, but the night experience was a different story. Having never landed on an aircraft carrier at night, I was extremely nervous as I prepared for my approach. The night was black with low clouds, drizzle and a strong 45-knot headwind. At 10 miles from the carrier I was in the landing configuration, gear and flaps down, and my landing hook was down, ready for the arrestment. At three miles I left 1,200 feet on my decent to the carrier landing area, at two miles I was at 800 feet, and at one mile I was at 400 feet.

Everything looked good as I approached the ship. At three quarters of a mile I was looking at the ship in good shape to land. The landing lens was correct with the meatball centered. The landing area was dimly lit. The Landing Signal Officer (LSO), positioned on the back of ship to help guide pilots to a safe landing, acknowledged on the radio that I was in good shape, but warned me of the 45 knots of wind across the deck (25 to 30 knots was normal). I was on speed at 140 knots. Then, just before I crossed the round down (the back of the ship), I focused on the landing area and not on the landing lens, known as "spotting the deck." Suddenly, I began a huge sink rate. The LSO frantically yelled on the radio, "POWER, POWER, POWER, POWER, WAVE OFF, WAVE OFF! YOU ARE TOO LOW!"

I went to full power, then full afterburner, but my aircraft continued to sink. I don't exactly know how, but miraculously I got over the round down and landed, snagging the number-one arresting cable (number three of four cables is the optimum cable to snag). After the arrestment I taxied out of the landing area and was sent to the catapult for takeoff to attempt another landing. My heart was racing, I was sweating, and I could feel every beat of my heart as it pounded relentlessly in my head. I asked myself how I ever got myself into this position. Nothing like a near ramp strike to take a man's bravado down a notch or two!

After a couple minutes I was shot off the end of the ship and back into the landing pattern in the blackness of the night sky. My next two night landings were much better, but I was still shaking from the first attempt. After three night landings I parked and shut down my aircraft on the carrier for the night. I walked into the Ready Room. I sat down and wondered how close I came to death that night. Little did I know that "near death" hovered over me in future aviation situations in my military career.

The next morning the LSO, Major Scotty Dudley, talked to me about the night before. He took me up on the flight deck and we walked to the back of the ship where he showed me where my arresting hook hit the round down. I looked in disbelief as I saw the huge horse print that the hook made on the round down. The hook should hit the flight deck roughly 175 to 200 feet past the round down (stern). My attempt for a carrier arrested landing was unacceptable. He looked at me and said, "Never, ever, ever get that low again, or your flying days will be over."

That was all I had to see and hear, I never again got that close to the end of the ship. That day I finished up with my day and night carrier landings and qualified for carrier duty before flying back to MCAS El Toro. I was a little more humble and a lot more experienced.

After carrier qualification, I was sent immediately to MCAS Iwakuni, Japan, where our four-plane detachment was formed and commanded by Major Bill "Basic" Beam. Besides Major Beam, our pilots were Captain Tim "Sniper" Ghormley, First Lieutenant Bob "Rags" Pearson and yours truly, First Lieutenant Greg "Snake" Raths. Our detachment was designated VMFP-3 Detachment 2, and after a couple weeks to get adjusted to the western Pacific region and time zone we flew aboard the USS Midway and joined Carrier Air Wing 5 in the Sea of Japan. The Air Wing comprised of two F-4J squadrons, two A-7E squadrons, one A-6E and KA-6D squadron, a detachment of four EA-6B Prowlers, a detachment of four E-2B Hawkeyes, four SH-3G helicopters plus our detachment of four RF-4Bs. We had a great crew, and we were ready for anything.

CHAPTER 26

Living on an aircraft carrier was a whole new experience for me. As a junior officer I had to learn to survive in very tight quarters. I was assigned to a 12-man bunkroom with six bunks and a bathroom across the hallway. Commanded by Navy Captain T.F. Brown, III, our carrier, the Midway, was manned by over 4,500 sailors and Marines. The Air Wing was CVW-5, the nation's only "911" air wing, a critical combat strike element of Battle Force Seventh Fleet, the only forward-deployed carrier strike group in the U.S. Navy.

On April 9, 1979, our Carrier Battle Group rushed to the Indian Ocean and Arabian Sea. We were responding to the crisis in Iran when the pro-western Shah left Iran for exile earlier that year. With the resulting power vacuum the Ayatollah Khomeini returned to Tehran. The royal regime collapsed shortly after when guerrillas and rebels overwhelmed troops that were loyal to the Shah in armed street fighting. It was a frightening time for those in Iran, and they voted by national referendum to become an Islamic Republic and to approve a new theocratic constitution, whereby Khomeini became Supreme Leader of the country.

The Midway Battle Group patrolled the waters near Iran

for three months before being relieved by another battle group. In mid-April we sailed home to Japan after port visits in Mombasa, Kenya, Perth, Australia and Subic Bay in the Philippines. One day I have etched in my brain is April 18, 1979. That is the day I became a member of the "Domain of Neptunus Rex," when aboard the USS Midway at Latitude 00-00, Longitude 83 degrees 56' E, I appeared into the Royal Domain and having been inspected and found worthy by the Royal Staff, was initiated into the Mysteries of the Ancient Order of the Deep and received my certificate as a "Trusty Shellback." Although all Navy and Marine Corps personnel know what this means, let me explain to my lay readers. Whenever a U.S. Navy ship crosses the equator, all crewmembers that have never crossed the equator before on a Navy ship are initiated with some juvenile stunts, like sitting in a box full of garbage, or being paraded on the flight deck like elephants holding on to the person ahead with heads down. These new recruits are called "pollywogs" until initiation is complete. A good soaking by fire crews with their large hoses ends the initiates with fun had by all.

Perth is a beautiful city that welcomed U.S. military men with open arms. Hundreds of the city's citizens came out to meet us as we came ashore, and many families opened their homes to the American Sailors and Marines. The Australian people are still very grateful for the American military support during World War II. I found a hotel room at the Sheraton with a big, soft bed that didn't roll back and forth all day and night, and I slept for 12 hours straight. Our stay in Perth was only four days and then back aboard ship to our next port visit in the Philippines to offload weapons. What a tropical paradise it was in the Philippines, with afternoon rain showers followed by baking sunshine. It was a great place to unwind with an ice-cold San Miguel beer at Peso Jimmy's in Olongapo City. The nightclubs had Filipino bands playing classic rock and roll. I sat at the bar and listened to the music, drank a few beers and relaxed with my buddies. It was almost like I was on vacation.

After the Philippines, we sailed north for Japan, and once we were back in the Sea of Japan we flew our aircraft off to MCAS Iwakuni. The USS Midway continued to cruise further north to the shipyard in Yokosuka to dock. Once back in Iwakuni, we flew land-based missions during our final two months there. A few weeks before leaving, we flew to Osan Air Force Base in the Republic of Korea (ROK), located about 40 miles south of Seoul, where we participated in an exercise with the Korean Air Forces to run through our air defenses against a possible invasion from the north. The exercise was intense, but I enjoyed visiting Korea and spending time with the Korean Air Force pilots.

My deployment overseas was very special. The flying was great and I was able to see a lot of different cultures and learned about different customs. In August 1979 I headed back to MCAS El Toro and rejoined my squadron in southern

California. Once I was back stateside, a squadron mate, First Lieutenant Bruce "Lash Larue" Paul and I purchased a small three-bedroom home in Mission Viejo, a small community south of the base. Our house soon earned the reputation as "The Snake Pit" because of parties we threw. On weekends our place was full of pilots and unknown women from as far away as Yuma. Although I missed my place near the beach, this home was ours and it felt good to be a homeowner. I felt like a full-fledged adult, well almost an adult… I'll leave it at that. It was time for more responsibilities.

Back at the squadron I began to train as a Landing Signal Officer (LSO) to help train our new pilots for carrier duty. I would sit on the end of the runway in a truck while the pilots would practice their touch-and-go landings. I had a radio so I could talk to the pilots and give them help if they were having trouble. I graded each landing approach and would later debrief the pilots on their trends. I soon began the process to get my squadron's LSO certification. I worked with the experienced Navy LSOs, at the Naval Air Station, Miramar in San Diego. After the training in San Diego was complete, I flew out to the aircraft carrier USS Coral Sea (CV-43), and waved different aircraft both day and night. I was certified in December 1979. I was climbing the military ladder and loving it.

During a training flight over the desert of Arizona near Yuma I was engaged in an air-to-air aerial dogfight with another F-4. I was practicing the last-ditch maneuver as the Phantom closed into guns' range behind me. I pulled back on the stick with all my strength to avoid the (simulated) gun shots and the next thing I knew I felt a snap in my neck as I pulled way too many Gs and blacked out. The officer in my back seat, Major Cooper, sustained the G forces without blacking out. Good thing. He sensed that I had because the aircraft was out of control and spiraling in a hard turn toward the earth. He began yelling through the intercom, "FORWARD STICK, FORWARD STICK, FORWARD STICK," trying to get me to subconsciously release the pressure I still had on the flight controls, thereby release the number of Gs and bring me back to consciousness. I faintly heard his screaming and released the stick pressure as the blood rushed back into my head. Luck was definitely on my side that day. I regained consciousness as the aircraft was passing through 8,000 feet. I leveled the wings and pulled back on the stick to avoid the ground by just a couple of thousand feet.

Major Cooper and I began communicating again. I was okay. My neck was stiff and I was breathing hard, but I was alive and so was he. I looked down at the G meter in my cockpit and it was pegged past 10 Gs. This was not good; the F-4 is built to withstand Gs of around 7 to 8. Whew! With MCAS Yuma nearby, I set up for a straight in approach and landed safely. The aircraft was out of commission for several days, but after extensive inspections it was certified airworthy again. I had to go through some centrifuge G testing before I could fly again, but it went well and I was back in the sky in a couple of short weeks. I had already used two of my nine lives. I was beginning to keep count, but I was young and unafraid. "Death, you want me? I can beat you each time," I recall thinking.

In February 1980, I was selected to attend an eight-week course at MCAS Yuma, Arizona to become my squadron's Weapons and Tactics Instructor (WTI). The course was taught by the Marine Aviation Weapons and Tactics Squadron One (MAWTS-1). MAWTS-1 provided standardized advanced tactical training and certification of unit instructor qualifications that support Marine aviation training and readiness and to provide assistance in the development and employment of aviation weapons and tactics. This designation enabled me to become my squadron's pilot training officer (PTO) and work in the squadron's operations department. This position allowed me to train the younger pilots for combat and carrier duty.

CHAPTER 27

On August 1, 1980 I was at the El Toro Officer's Club having a few beers with my squadron mates watching some exotic dancers in the back room (you don't see that anymore at military clubs) when a pilot from another squadron walked up to me and asked how I'd been doing. He was Captain Dick Hubbard, an A6-E pilot I knew from WTI in Yuma. After some small talk, he asked me if I wanted to meet his girlfriend's roommate who was in the front room of the club. Her name was Luci Novotny, and she'd recently moved to California from North Carolina. Dick introduced me to her and we danced a bit. I took her phone number and we began dating a couple of weeks later.

As I got to know Luci I learned that she had a 4-year-old son named Michael and a former husband, Marine Corps Captain Michael Novotny, who had died in an A-6E accident in 1978. I had heard about that accident. Novotny's aircraft impacted the ground during a night training mission in North Carolina in November of '78. The other member in the aircraft was Captain Lee Barthel, an officer I knew from flight school. Luci and I had a few things in common. On a positive note, we shared a few good commonalities. We were both Catholic, the same age, knew about Marine Corps aviation, and we were both very easy going. My concern was whether she was willing to date another aviator. That concern faded as our relationship blossomed and I hit it off with her son. He was a great kid who was looking for a father figure. I decided to take the relationship day by day, but after a couple months we were a couple.

Luci was originally from western Pennsylvania. She grew up just east of Pittsburgh and attended Indiana University of Pennsylvania, where she earned her B.S. in Elementary Education. She had older siblings, Sam and Linda. Her parents, Salvatore (Sam) and Elsie Fanelli, were second-generation Italian Americans. Luci met her husband during college, married him and went with him to Pensacola, Florida, where he attended flight school. After flight training he was assigned to MCAS Cherry Point, North Carolina. Luci moved with him. Little Michael was born on October 13, 1976. Luci's husband died just two years later. Having such a great childhood, it made me sad to think that this boy would never remember his father. When Luci's husband died, Luci decided to come out to California to start a new life with her son.

Things between Luci and I were going real well until I was selected to go back overseas to the USS Midway for another six-month carrier cruise. That was in November 1980. We had to put our relationship on hold for awhile. Luci and Michael flew to Japan to spend some time with me during Christmas and lived in the Officer's Quarters with me for a couple of weeks. This arrangement wouldn't work out long term. Michael was getting to an age where he was a handful. Luci asked me if I would help her with him, and I tried my best to be a good role model. I disciplined him from time to time. Children need rules and boundaries. It was amazing to see the change in this kid. He went from being hardheaded to a really nice kid in short time. All it took was time and directed discipline. I was good in that role. I was, after all, very disciplined myself. One has to be in order to be a jet pilot. Luci was grateful, and the bond between us grew. We were becoming a family. Everything in my life seemed to be changing.

President Reagan was sworn in as our 40th President in January1981, and he made good on his promise to rebuild the U.S. military. He initially gave us a 14% pay increase and began modernizing the military, from the M-16 rifle to the largest battle ship. His administration poured billions of dollars into the military coffers. After four years of tight and restrictive defense budgets under President Carter, President Reagan made it his priority to help the military to once again be an effective world military force. A sad commentary to this point was when I was off the coast of Iran in 1979 and the Shah was deposed, the Iranian Air Force was flying the modern sophisticated F-14 Tomcats they had purchased from the United States while we were still flying the 25-year-old F-4 Phantom II. President Reagan swore this would never happen again and took up the slogan, "Peace through Strength." His full court press to update the military caught the Soviets off guard who were ahead in the arms race, but the United States soon regained its premier military dominance in the world.

The pilots on my deployment were Major John Laurent, Captain Bob Pearson, First Lieutenant Reed Olson and me, now a Captain. Our four-plane detachment was VMFP-3 Det Bravo. While preparing for the cruise and flying field carrier landing practice (FCLP) at the Iwakuni Air Base, I had just lifted off from a touch and go and I smelled smoke in the cockpit. I turned downwind to set up for another landing when the electrical system of the aircraft failed and black smoked billowed from the rear seat. The backup electrical system also failed when I deployed the ram air turbine (RAT). I watched in disbelief as the entire cockpit filled with a dense black smoke.

I had to think fast, so I pulled the air vent system handle to help release the smoke from the cockpit. It worked for the front seat, but not so much in the back seat where Major Marty Bender was seated. Fire and smoke were all around him. I had no radios to talk to the tower, my flaps had blown up with no electrical power to keep them down, and I had to fly by the seat of my pants to get this burning aircraft back on the ground. The only instrument that was working was the airspeed indicator that functioned off ram air into a small pitot tube on the nose of the aircraft. There was no time for me to lose my head if I wanted to save our lives. I briefly considered pulling the ejection handle to get us both out of the burning jet, but then I had a gut feeling that I could get this aircraft on the ground safely

I increased my airspeed to take into account the extra airspeed I needed with no flaps, turned onto final and headed for the landing area. I lowered my arresting hook to try to catch a cable strung across the runway for just such emergencies. Major Bender had his mask on tight so he could breathe even though he couldn't see through the smoke. He later told me that he was fine, because he sensed that I had the aircraft under control. With no communication with the tower I took it upon myself to get this aircraft on the ground immediately, so I touched down and took the arresting cable and the aircraft came to a stop. I secured the engines; we opened our canopies, unstrapped, and leapt out of the smoking jet. Major Bender was pretty shook up and was coughing up smoke. We were both taken to the base hospital for treatment, and later released. We were fine physically, but Major Bender decided to never fly again. We both were awarded the Navy Commendation Medal for our actions during that flight. Hmm, life number three; six to go! Maybe I should start taking these life-threatening events a little more seriously. Should I consider switching professions?? Nope! Get me back into a cockpit.

With this aircraft severely damaged, our RF-4B detachment went on cruise with only three planes. We flew the three aircraft onboard the USS Midway on February 8, 1981, and we set sail for the Arabian Sea. We stopped in Singapore for a three-day port visit before we entered the Indian Ocean. Singapore is a bustling metropolis with large high-rise buildings that touched the sky. I was awestruck as I looked up the sides of these buildings. The food was different, but I was willing to try everything once. No regrets.

After the port visit, it was back to work flying training missions on the way to the Persian Gulf. Once in the Arabian Sea we set up combat patrols and reconnaissance flights to keep an eye on the Iranians and other trouble spots in the area, such as Yemen and Oman. On March 30, 1981, I had just returned from a flight when I heard the news that President Reagan was shot, just 69 days into his presidency. While leaving a speaking engagement at the Washington Hilton Hotel in Washington, D.C., President Reagan and three others were wounded by John Hinckley, Jr. President Reagan suffered a punctured lung, but prompt medical attention allowed him to recover quickly. We in the military were glad he recovered and remained our Commander-in-Chief. The nation as a whole seemed relieved.

While in the Indian Ocean we received intelligence that the new Soviet aircraft carrier "Minsk" was in the area. I was given a mission to find the carrier and report back to the Midway its speed and direction. For three weeks we could not locate the Soviet carrier. One afternoon I flew about 300 miles from the Midway tracking a radar signal I had picked up, hoping it may be the Minsk. On the horizon, I caught sight of this mammoth 42,000-ton ship, powered by 4-shaft geared steam turbines. I caught them off guard as I flew up the starboard (right) side of the carrier taking multiple pictures and getting all the intelligence data requested. They quickly turned their gun turrets at me and began launching their YAK-38 fighter aircraft. I think I got enough pictures; time to get out of dodge and back to the Midway, I thought. I climbed up to altitude and reported in code what I had located and gave the Midway the Minsk's position, speed and direction. With two YAK-38s on my tail I put my aircraft engines into afterburner and they soon broke off and went back to their ship. Wow, that was exciting for a young Captain. I felt like the young pilot from the movie Midway when he spotted the Japanese Fleet. After landing the photos were developed and there in beautiful black and white was the Soviet carrier we had been looking for weeks.

After this event it was time to return to Japan. Luci and I kept in touch with each other while I was away. The Midway would receive mail about once a week from a C-2 cargo aircraft out of Diego Garcia, a small British-owned island in the Indian Ocean. We would number our letters so we knew the order to open them if we received several letters at a time. On June 28, 1981, I returned home to California. Luci and Michael were there waiting for me. I don't think I'd ever been so happy to see familiar faces. I had missed them terribly. Our relationship withstood the six-month separation and we easily picked up where we had left off.

Christmas 1981, was at my parents' house in Phoenix, and
I brought Luci and Michael to participate in all the events.
Luci and I were engaged the month prior and we set March
6, 1982, as our wedding date. We would get married at St.
Gregory's Catholic Church in Phoenix, where Bishop Thomas
O'Brien would perform the Mass and marriage ceremony. He
was assisted by Father Bob Skagen, my good friend from St.
Gregory's, and my math teacher from Bourgade, Father Jim
Rodenspiel. Nick Ganem was my best man, and my brothers
Bob and Steve, along with my cousin Jim Jorgensen, were the
groomsmen. Luci's sister Linda Farrell was matron of honor
and Luci's good friends Randi Weber, Barb Hubbard and Anne
Zimmer were her bridesmaids. Luci wore a beautiful, long
wedding gown that made her look like a princess. Mike was in
a miniature tuxedo and was our ring boy (24 years earlier, in
the same church, I was the ring boy for my Aunt and Uncle).
That memory went through my mind as I watched Mike walk
up to the altar with the ring pillow. I was decked out in my
military dress blue uniform. A large grin swept over my face
when Luci came down the aisle with her father. I felt blessed.

The reception was at a nice hotel ballroom near the church.
Several of my Marine Corps buddies showed up along with
my family and friends from Phoenix. The reception concluded
with my Marine pals throwing me into the hotel swimming
pool in my dress blues. Did I expect anything less? Luci wasn't

at all thrilled with my friends, but she knew how Marines could get with some alcohol in their bellies.

I bought out my roommate's portion of the Mission Viejo house, and Luci and Michael moved in with me. I now had my own little family. The house had a swimming pool in the backyard where Michael loved to swim and play. We bought him a Cocker Spaniel we named Freddie, after Freddie Lynn of the California Angels. Luci did some remodeling to the house: new carpet, paint, wallpaper, furniture, tile and other accessories. Any resemblance to the former bachelor pad was gone. Luci even got rid of my favorite green plaid reclining chair that I bought on the side of the road in Virginia. The Snake Pit was officially closed. The Raths Family Home now took its place.

One afternoon when Luci and I were on a walk, a neighbor met us and said, "Thank goodness those Marines moved out of that house. They were a wild bunch of boys." Little did that neighbor know that I was one of those boys. I just smiled politely and agreed with her.

A few months after the wedding, Luci announced that she was pregnant. I had recently adopted Mike and he took my last name, and our little family was now going to get a bit larger. We were all excited about the baby. Luci's pregnancy was progressing well, and one day while I was at work, she called me from the doctor's office, where she just had a sonogram. She asked me, "Are you sitting down?"

"Why, what's wrong?"

"We're having twins!"

"TWINS? Oh... my." That's all I could say at that moment.

On May 12th, 1983, Luci gave birth to our daughters, Kristen and Kathryn. In just 14 months, I had gained a wife and three children. My world had changed forever, but changed for the better. I was one very happy husband and father.

Back at the squadron, our intelligence department received word from Washington, D.C., that Fidel Castro was up to no good again. There was some construction on the east side of the Cuban Island and American intelligence was concerned, especially after what happened in 1962 when Castro received nuclear missiles and launchers from Premier Khrushchev's Soviet Union.

Our squadron dispatched four RF-4Bs to Key West, Florida, to prepare for reconnaissance mission around the communist island. I was one of the pilots to go on the deployment and I was excited to fly some real world missions again. Each day we would take off from the Naval Air Station in Key West and fly around the island to take pictures. After the mission we would land at the U.S. Naval Station at Guantanamo Bay to refuel and debrief our mission. Guantanamo Bay is 45 square miles of U.S. territory located in the Oriente Province on the southeast corner of Cuba; the base is about 400 air miles from Miami.

There was also some suspicious activity along the fence line that separated U.S. territory and Cuban territory around the base, so after taking off from Gitmo, we took photographs along the fence line. On our way back to Key West while flying in international airspace, my wingman, Chuck "Overstress" Strong, sited two Soviet built MIG-21 fighter aircraft coming our way off our left side. Even though we were not carrying any air-to-air missiles, Stress called for a tactical turn into them to scare them back into their airspace. Hmm... was this a smart move? Were we playing chicken with two MIGS loaded with air-to-air missiles? Before I could answer those questions the MIGs turned and hightailed it back into Cuban airspace. Whew!

Back in Key West the intelligence folks were having trouble determining if the construction site on the island was some kind of missile site installation. Conducting our missions in international airspace made it difficult to get a good picture, even with our state-of-the-art cameras. The Admiral in charge of intelligence came up to me and said he wanted a clearer picture. "Do you want me to fly into Cuban airspace to get the picture, Admiral?" I asked.

"No, no, no. That could start an international incident" he replied. "But it sure would be nice to see what that site is," he continued. Was he asking me indirectly to fly into Cuban airspace and get the photo? Well, then, what would I do?

On my next mission as a young Captain I decided to take the

chance of getting shot down and fly over the island to get the picture. I flew out at sea for a few miles and dropped down to about 100 feet over the water and turned toward the island. Kicking in the afterburners, I reached a speed of 650 knots and went over Cuba and headed directly to the site. Once I acquired the site I popped up to about 500 feet and started the cameras rolling, then back down as low as I could get until I got back into international airspace. Wow, the adrenalin was flowing through my body like red hot chili pepper sauce as I climbed to altitude and headed back to Key West. The film was developed, and the Admiral got what he needed. Nothing was ever said, until now, 30 years later. I would have to assume that the construction site was not a concern to our country's national security since nothing ever transpired after my mission.

Back home, in July 1983, just as the twins turned two months, I received a call from the officer in charge of military orders who informed me that I had been selected to attend the Amphibious Warfare School (AWS), a nine-month course at Quantico, Virginia, providing career-level professional military education. The school prepares Marine Captains to function as commanders and staff officers at appropriate levels within the Operating Forces and Supporting Establishment. Although, honored to be selected for this education opportunity, the orders were to begin in August, which meant a cross-country move with two infants, a 6-year-old boy and a dog. It was all a bit overwhelming. We had to get packing and fast.

A moving company packed up our belongings for us, which took some of the pressure off. I rented out our beautiful home; we loaded our two vehicles and strapped the babies into their car seats as we headed for Virginia. We had an Oldsmobile Cutlass and a Ford F-150 pickup truck. Luci drove the Cutlass, and I took the truck. We only drove a 100 miles on our first day and had to stop in Palms Springs for the night. The twins were not doing well with the travel, so we bedded down early for the evening. We found a pet-friendly hotel and I ordered two cribs to be sent to the room. I always enjoyed watching the expressions of the delivery staff. It was as if we had made a mistake by ordering two.

Our next stop would be Phoenix, a 250-mile journey. I put the two car seats in my truck and took the twins for this leg of the trip. Luci had Mike and the dog. We made good time, but the twins had been crying almost the whole time. They stopped crying as we pulled into my parents' driveway that evening. This was not going to work. At this pace it would take weeks to reach Virginia. Time for Plan B. Luci would fly to her parents' house in Pennsylvania from Phoenix with the twins and wait for me there. Brother Bob would drive her car, and I would take Mike and the dog in the truck. Once in Pennsylvania Bob would fly home. Plan B went well except for the four-hour plane ride Luci had to endure with the babies. Airline passengers quickly changed seats. Luci ended up alone in the front of the plane with two crying babies. Luci looked a wreck at the end of that flight.

It took some getting used to, but we eventually settled into our base housing unit in Quantico, and I started my schooling in August. We were both drained from the trip, but slowly we got into a routine. Mike went to school at a base elementary school. When Christmas came around we drove to Pennsylvania and stayed with Luci's parents for the holidays. Her mother loved taking care of our little girls, and Mike and grandpa were best of buddies. We enjoyed the break from the daily duties. With our twins, it was always something it seemed.

In January of 1984, both girls came down with pneumonia and we rushed them to the hospital. They were admitted for three days of observation and treatment. This reminded me of my bout with pneumonia when I was a baby. They both pulled through with flying colors, and though I probably shouldn't admit it, there was an upside. Luci and I got three nights of sleep at home with no baby feedings or diaper changing!

I completed my schooling in May 1984 and received orders back to MCAS El Toro, California, so now we had to drive across country again. This time the twins were 14 months old and handled the trip much better. After nine stops along the way, we pulled back into our driveway of our Mission Viejo home and I checked back into my squadron.

Luci went to work as a fifth-grade teacher at Immaculate Heart School in Santa Ana. Mike went to the same school, and we found a nice young lady to take care of the twins during the day. It was now time to find a larger home. We found a four-bedroom, three-bath home with a swimming pool and a great view of the Saddleback Valley in a newer section of Mission Viejo. The home had a huge bonus room for the children to play in upstairs. My sister-in-law, Birda, came for a visit and taught the twins to swim. I put a fence around the pool for additional safety. It didn't take us long to adjust to the home.

I was back flying the RF-4B at the squadron and returned to my position as pilot training officer. We had a few small deployments around the country, but for the most part I got to stay home. This was important to me since the children were still very young. On one particular squadron deployment, when our squadron was flying to Florida for some training with the Navy, we stopped at the Naval Air Station in Dallas to refuel. Our squadron had just received a new commanding officer, LtCol Sperry, and he was with us on the trip. The weather in Dallas was raining with low-hanging dark clouds. After we all refueled the first two aircraft to take off were piloted by Major Hill and LtCol Sperry. As they entered the dark clouds, LtCol Sperry lost sight of Major Hill, and within seconds they had a midair collision. LtCol Sperry's aircraft was severely damaged and he had to eject. His aircraft crashed into an unpopulated area. LtCol Sperry and the officer in the back seat, Major Fagan, were both uninjured as they safely parachuted to earth, landing on a golf course. The other aircraft involved in the mishap was damaged, but was able to return and land safely back at Dallas. I had yet to takeoff.

When I figured out what had happened, I shook my head, returned to the flight line, shut down my aircraft and got out of my jet. The next day, the Commanding General of the Third Marine Aircraft Wing relieved LtCol Sperry of his command and replaced him with LtCol Foss. Needless to say, the deployment to Florida was a somber time.

After we returned from Florida our squadron returned to normal operations and everything was going well. But in May of 1985, I was told that I was being transferred to Japan again for a year. The deployment would be unaccompanied, meaning the military would not pay to bring my family with me. I was really disappointed since we had moved into our new house less than a year earlier and I would be leaving my family behind.

I hatched a plan. I would bring my family to Japan and, at my own expense, rent a home for them near the base. I could live there with them for the summer, giving me three months with my family before they would have to go back home for school. Mike, then 8 years old, wanted to stay with Luci's parents in Pennsylvania for the summer. So much for the plan. At least part of it would work.

I found a furnished house for the summer, and two weeks after I arrived in Japan, Luci and the girls joined me. Mike flew to Pittsburgh for summer fun with his grandparents and cousins. Luci and our 2-year-old girls flew into Tokyo, and then took a train to the base, where I was waiting for them with hugs and the biggest smile ever. I bought a used Japanese mini-van that we called the "bongo van," and we all settled in for the summer.

My squadron was no longer attached to the USS Midway, so we stayed in Iwakuni for the summer, flying training flights over Japan, Korea, and the Philippine Islands. Luci and the girls would come on base to use the swimming pool, recreation facilities and Officer's Club. On weekends we toured around southern Japan. We visited Hiroshima, the city that took the brunt of the first nuclear bomb during World War II, and I was happy to see that it was booming again after so much devastation.

CHAPTER 28

On July 3, 1985, I received devastating news in the form of a telegram telling me that my good friend Jimmy O'Connor had been killed in an automobile accident. He was coming home from a softball game, lost control of his Bronco and went down an embankment in Canada where he was then living. He didn't make it to the hospital. He left behind his wife Kathy and three young children, Paul, Erin and Julie. I was unable to make it back for the funeral, but his death had a profound effect on me. The news rocked the O'Connor clan and brought us all to the reality on how fragile our lives are. Jim was only 33 years old. I still keep in touch with Jim's siblings and children. Most of them live in Phoenix and we get together for an annual memorial golf tournament to honor Jim, his dad and two uncles.

As the summer was coming to an end, Luci had met some Department of Defense (DoD) teachers who taught at the base school, Matthew C. Perry Elementary School, and they said they were looking for a teacher. Luci talked with the principal who was willing to hire her for the school year to teach first grade. After we discussed the situation, we decided to stay as a family for the rest of the year in Japan. The people renting our house in Mission Viejo agreed to stay until we got back, and Luci contacted her parents to get Mike a passport and an airline ticket to Tokyo. I was able to get an extension on the lease on our house in Japan, and then flew to Tokyo to pick up Mike. I had my whole family together again. Mike, then 8 years old, was a real trooper, flying from Pittsburgh to Los Angeles and then on to Tokyo on his own. That's a long flight for anyone. Mike enrolled in the fourth grade at Perry School, and Kristen and Kathy stayed at the base childcare center during the day. Life was good for all of us. Things must have been too calm, because it was time to test my lifesaving skills again. Now, with a family, I didn't need Mr. Death anywhere around me, but here he came again.

In October, 1985, I was taxiing my aircraft to the runway for takeoff at Iwakuni when I smelled a foul odor in the cockpit. It smelled like smoke from an electrical fire, but I dismissed it; then the smell grew more intense. From my earlier experience with an aircraft fire my instinct was to get the heck out of this aircraft and fast. A quick radio message to tower notifying them of my problem, I shut down both engines, opened the canopy, unstrapped and hurried out of the aircraft. As I did so, I noticed flames coming from under the ejection seat. I hastened my exit.

Just as I was climbing down onto the wing, the front cockpit ejection seat cooked off from the intense heat and shot out of the aircraft, smashing the open canopy. Pieces of Plexiglas hit me on the back of my helmet as I slid off the wing onto the tarmac. The officer in the rear seat, Major Burton, experienced burns to his face as he exited the aircraft. Within seconds after we got out of the aircraft, the entire cockpit was ablaze. Flames leapt over ten feet from the cockpit as the crash crew pulled up to the scene. They extinguished the fire as quickly as they could as we were loaded into an ambulance. Another trip to the hospital, but we were okay and released back into our natural habitat. At this point in my life I had now faced Mr. Death four times in an aircraft, with me prevailing on each occasion. But now, with a family, I found myself taking back my earlier no fear comments. Now it was, "Go find someone else to menace, Mr. Death. Just leave me alone."

After I was released from the hospital, I drove to the school where Luci was teaching and shared the news about my close call. I didn't want her to hear from anyone else. That night I hugged Luci and the children and we said our prayers together. I was truly thankful to be alive. I was thankful to have my little family.

Michael became involved in Cub Scouts on base and also joined a soccer team. It was fun to watch him play with the other players. I bought him a bike to get him to and from school from our house. It was sometimes like I was watching myself as a child, riding away from my house to whatever adventures lay ahead. Mike was a great big brother to the twins. They counted on him to help them around the house. Our family blended well in our Japanese neighborhood.

Although we knew little of the Japanese language, we always said hello to the neighbors or nodded to them. We never had to lock the doors of our house or van. There was absolutely no crime in the town where we lived. It was amazing to us.

When May 1986 came around, it was time for us to head back to California. Luci had finished teaching for the school year. Mike successfully completed the fourth grade, and we packed up for home. I was able to get my family on a military flight under "space available" that flew direct from Iwakuni to El Toro. After a long flight, with stops in Hawaii and Alaska, we landed safely back in California. It was so good to be back in our own home on our native turf.

I was just promoted to Major as we settled into our home to enjoy the California lifestyle again. Just as we were settling in, the officer in charge of military transfers (called a monitor) notified me and said orders were being delivered to me to go to Detroit for a three-year tour of duty. I was selected to command the Marine Corps Recruiting Station, headquartered in Detroit. My area would cover southern Michigan and northern Ohio. I would command 65 enlisted recruiters and two officer recruiters. Although it was an honor to be selected for command, I was not ready to pack up the family and move again. The Marine Corps wanted me in Detroit by August 1, which made my head spin. We'd only been back in California for two months. However, this was a great opportunity for me, because I had recently been promoted. This next move would further my career. After consulting Luci, we decided that I would head to Michigan alone. Luci would stay in California and try to sell our house. Once the house sold, she would bring the family to Michigan.

This move also meant I wouldn't be flying for three years. As a pilot, I was not thrilled with being out of the cockpit for so long, but I was promised orders to fly the new F/A-18 Hornet back in El Toro after the tour. In late July, I packed up my pickup truck and drove to Detroit. I rented a small apartment and began my assignment. The job was specific. My recruiting station needed to recruit an assigned number of qualified young men and women, age 18 to 27, into the Marine Corps each month. If my recruiters met their assigned monthly quota, I would be a hero, but if they missed the numbers, the District Commander and his team, headquartered in Kansas, would pay me a visit.

I was the fourth commanding officer (CO) of the Detroit Recruiting Station in the prior 14 months. Three previous COs were either relieved or left military service. I was the first aviator to be selected to command a recruiting station. Usually, the ground officers were chosen for this command, but they insisted that aviators help with such a difficult assignment. I immediately felt the pressure as soon as I arrived.

The station had not met its quota in over a year, and my Executive Officer (XO), Captain Steve Gilman, pulled me aside to explain the craziness of the job I just inherited. I was determined to get this place on track and produce positive results. After analyzing the demographics of my assigned recruiting area, I called in the recruiters and presented my plan to get the station generating recruits. I am a people person, and my strategy was to get to know each of my recruiters personally, and then determine their strengths and weaknesses. Then, I would place them in the areas where I thought they would do the best with the population. Simple enough, I thought.

I had 18 recruiting substations in my area, from Toledo, Ohio, to Port Huron, Michigan. At each substation I placed two or three recruiters, with a Staff Non-Commissioned Officer (SNCO) in charge of each substation. I used black recruiters in the inner city because they understood the black community, and I placed white recruiters in the suburbs. This was a business and to make it successful I needed such a strategy to make my numbers. Each recruiter knew my philosophy of leadership, and each went to work with a positive attitude.

My boss was not enthused with a pilot commanding one of his recruiting stations. Pilots had a reputation as being laid back, and the ground pounders had little use for pilots, unless we were providing close air support in a combat zone. With my family back in California, I put 100% of my time into getting my station functioning smoothly. The first month I took command we exceeded our numbers. Then the second month, then the third and then the fourth we exceeded quota.

Things were going very well and the recruiters finally believed in themselves. Headquarters was impressed and stayed out of my way.

While my wife was waiting to sell our house in California, I put money down on a new home under construction in the Clinton Township, about 20 miles north of Detroit. Completion date was set for January 1987, and I was hoping our house would sell by then or I would have to rent it. In November 1986, we accepted an offer on our house in California, and in mid-December I flew out to California to pack up Luci and the kids for our drive to Motown.

Unfortunately, construction on our new house was running behind schedule due to poor weather, so we had to live in my small apartment through April. Finally, in May, we moved into our newly built home in a beautiful area nestled among the tall trees of the Detroit outskirts. Our neighbors welcomed our family. They were Brad and Karen Johnston, Doug and Carol Harris, and Vito and Barbara LaPiccalo and their families, to name just a few. I'll never forget these people for their kindness and kinship. My children got along great with all the neighbor kids. Kristen and Kathy went to preschool at the nearby military base, Selfridge Air National Guard Base, and we enrolled Michael into the neighborhood middle school to finish fifth grade.

The 1987 Rose Bowl pitted The University of Michigan against my alma mater, Arizona State University. The entire state of Michigan anticipated an easy game against my Sun Devils. Local news and commentary praised coach Bo Schembechler, quarterback Jim Harbaugh and the Wolverines as an unbeatable team for the 73rd Annual Rose Bowl Classic. The Arizona State Sun Devils, champions of the Pacific-10 Conference, went on to defeat the Wolverines, champions of the Big Ten Conference, 22-15. It was a sweet victory for MY team. These were happy times, but even in the happiest there are sometimes dark clouds.

On January 31, 1987, Luci received a call from her sister informing her that her father had suffered a heart attack and died. We immediately packed up the car and drove to Pennsylvania for the funeral. Her father was only 69; his death came as an utter shock. Luci was heartbroken and I made it a priority to visit her mom as often as we could. The drive from Detroit to Pittsburgh took only a few hours. Mike took his grandfather's death very hard since the two of them were such good pals. He would have to adjust. Mike learned that year that death was indeed a part of life. He was waiting to come of age to go deer hunting with grandpa, but now those dreams were dashed. He missed his grandfather very much, but was a trooper through it all.

At the end of my first year in Detroit, everything was running smoothly. Luci was enjoying our new house, the kids were on summer break, the grass was green, the trees were full, and the long summer days brought warm sunshine. My neighbor,

Vito, was a local broadcaster for motor sports for the Detroit area and hosted a weekly radio show called Motor City Motor Sports. I was a big fan of Richard Petty, the NASCAR driver of the #43 STP stock car. Vito offered me a ticket to watch a NASCAR race at the Michigan International Speedway on a Sunday afternoon. Roger Penske owned the beautiful two-mile oval track in the Irish Hills of southeastern Michigan. On the Friday before the race, Vito took me to the track for media day and he was able to get me a ride in a stock car with NASCAR driver, Dick Trickle. I was impressed with the 200-mph speed the car made around the track. Also, on that day I got to ride in the pace car driven by the famous driver Dale Earnhardt, also known as the "Intimidator." I took my boy Mike to the Sunday race and Dale Earnhardt won it that day. I was now 100% hooked on NASCAR. Unfortunately in 2001, Dale Earnhardt experienced a horrific crash on the last turn of the final lap of the Daytona 500 and was killed. The entire racing world mourned.

As I reached the one-year mark on recruiting duty I could be very proud of my recruiting station, because we never missed quota. In fact, the station went from being the worst to the best in the 9th Marine Corps Recruiting District! Morale was high, and I had a well-lubricated train moving down the tracks. My second year on recruiting duty proved to be more difficult.

With an influx of new recruiters and the loss of some of my successful veteran recruiters, my station began to miss our quotas. The District dispatched their instructors to get us back on track. The current CO, Colonel Robert Lewis, (the last Marine Corps Officer to leave Vietnam) had me fly to Kansas City for a butt chewing and then sent me back to Detroit with half my butt gone. I swear my pants never fit the same after that. My station was also rocked by a recruiting scandal, where a local high school counselor was falsifying transcripts to help the less fortunate students start a new life in the military. We found eight such recruits that had to be discharged. Fortunately, it was proven that none of my recruiters were involved in the scandal.

My office was in downtown Detroit in a troubled section that was known for violence after dark. I always carried a 9 mm handgun in my briefcase for self-defense. One evening, as I was leaving the office on my way to the parking garage, two cars came racing around the corner at high speeds with tires screeching. Then I heard "pop, pop, pop... pop, pop" and then glass was shattering and people screaming. It only took me a split second to realize that I was in the middle of a gunfight between two gangs in cars. I hit the ground, opened my briefcase and pulled out my gun ready to do battle on the streets of Detroit. Loading a round in the chamber I took aim at the aggressor car where the gunfire was coming from, but before I could get off a shot they were well out of range. Seconds behind were several police cars with their sirens blaring and emergency lights lit up as they pursued the criminals. Dang, it felt like a combat zone. I learned the next morning that three gang members were killed during the shootout on the main drag, Jefferson Avenue. I downplayed the incident to Luci, but she was ready to get out of Detroit. "You are trained to do battle in foreign lands," she said. "Not on America's streets." She did have a good point. All I needed was a stray bullet to come my way, and it could have been lights out for Papa Greg.

It was now 1989 and I was now in my third and final year on recruiting duty. Mike was at Iroquis Middle School in Macomb, Michigan, and the twins were in kindergarten at Ojibwa Elementary School. Luci was working for a computer firm in a nearby town and she also worked part-time at Eastern Michigan University in Ypsilanti, supervising student teachers for the Education Department. My recruiting station improved and we were making quota again. Things were looking up as I counted down the final months in Michigan. Mike and I would attend Detroit Tiger baseball games and Red Wing hockey games when I had some free time. We even made it to a couple of Pistons' and Lions' games.. In the spring we put the house up for sale, and I received my transfer orders back to California to fly the F/A-18 Hornet. Our house sold quickly and it was now time to head back to the Golden State.

On July 6, 1989, at the Grosse Point War Memorial, on the beautiful shores of Lake St. Clair, I passed command of the recruiting station to Major John Dunn. The Marine Corps leadership was impressed with my tour and awarded me the

Meritorious Service Medal for excellence. My dad had flown out for the ceremony and beamed as Colonel Lewis pinned the medal to my uniform. With both of our vehicles packed up, and after a short reception at the War Memorial, Luci and I started our engines and put Detroit in our rearview mirrors as fast as we could. My dad drove back with us, and we dropped him off in Phoenix before heading back to our beloved southern California.

I checked into the Marine Corps Air Station in El Toro, and was told I would be sent to the Naval Air Station in Lemoore, California, for F/A-18 flight training. This base was about three hours north of Los Angeles. The training would take up to six months, but we decided to keep the family in El Toro during my training. I was able to drive home every weekend to be with my family, but with me being away all week placed a huge burden on Luci. She found a job teaching at St. Justin Martyr Catholic School in Anaheim, where the twins went with her for school. Michael attended Los Alisos Middle School in Mission Viejo. He became more and more interested in baseball and joined the local baseball league. During tryouts, a coach named Brian Griffen noticed Mike's ability to hit the ball and drafted him immediately. Mike became a starter and played for a couple years on his team. I was one proud papa! His coach, Brian and I are still friends to this day.

CHAPTER 29

After three years out of the cockpit, it would be a challenge to get back up and into the air again. This new aircraft was head and shoulders above the aging F-4 Phantom II that I had flown and knew so well. Made of a composite fiber that weighs much less than the F-4, this new plane had greater maneuverability. Plus, because it was powered by two masterful afterburning jet engines this aircraft had massive thrust in the hands of its pilot. The F/A-18 Hornet is a fourth generation air-to-air fighter and air-to-ground bomber with a Gatling gun in the nose for either air gunnery or ground strafing. I need to get my confidence back to take this jet on!

Each week that I flew the aircraft I could feel my confidence returning. My training concluded in March 1990 with aircraft carrier qualifications on the USS Ranger (CV-61). I completed 10 day landings and six night landings over a four-day period, and now I was certified to fly the F/A-18 in a fleet squadron. What a thrill flying would be now.

When I returned to MCAS El Toro a friend, Major Tim "Yogi" Hughes, was just leaving his position as the Commanding Officer of the Marine Headquarters Squadron for Marine Aircraft Group 11 (MAG-11). Tim recommended me for the job. The Group CO, Colonel Manfred "Fokker" Rietsch, offered me Yogi's position. I jumped at the chance and loved the job. Assigned to fly with Marine Fighter Attack Squadron 314 (VMFA-314), the Black Knights, one of seven F/A-18 squadrons in the air group, was an honor that I never saw coming. I remain grateful to this day.

In May 1990, Luci and I found our dream home in Mission Viejo. We had been looking to purchase a home, and this house was only about four years old, it had a beautiful swimming pool, four large bedrooms and a three-car garage. I had saved the money for a down payment, so we could sign the papers immediately and move in. The kids each had his/her own bedroom, and they couldn't get enough of the pool. I felt like I was living my dream. I had arrived.

I really enjoyed training with VMFA-314. The squadron's Operations Officer, Major Bob "Boomer" Knutzen, who was married to one of Luci's good friends, kept me on the flight schedule as much as possible. He knew I needed as much experience as possible to keep me current in the Hornet. Flying with the Black Knights helped sharpen my skills as a fighter/attack pilot. I didn't know just how handy that would be not too far in the future.

In the summer of 1990 Iraq accused Kuwait of stealing Iraqi petroleum through slant drilling, and the Iraqi dictator, Saddam Hussein, was making plans to attack the small Arab oil-rich country. After a grueling ten-year war with Iran, Hussein was unable to pay more than $80 billion that he had borrowed to finance the Iran-Iraq War. I will never forget the events that lead to my deployment for the next phase of this war.

As I lie in bed watching television on the evening of August 2, 1990, I was jolted out of my comfort zone when I heard a special report that the Iraqi Republican Guard had crossed the border into Kuwait and attacked the small nation. The invasion force of 120,000 troops and 2,000 tanks quickly overwhelmed Kuwait, allowing Hussein to declare, in less than a week, that Kuwait was his nation's nineteenth province. Oh, God, I thought. Here it comes.

The United Nations responded quickly, passing a series of resolutions that condemned the invasion, called for an immediate withdrawal of Iraqi troops from Kuwait, imposed a financial and trade embargo on Iraq, and declared the annexation void.

This was not good, I thought. The next morning, when I arrived at the El Toro base, we had a secret meeting to review the war plans for this specific circumstance. I could feel it in my stomach. I would be heading out yet again and this time, maybe because of the word "war," I was worried about the outcome. I had used up a few lives already.

Marine Aircraft Group 11 went immediately into combat planning. All of the squadrons were prepping their aircraft for combat, testing all the systems, changing out parts and hanging extra fuel tanks on the wings in preparation for a transatlantic crossing and future combat. Then the "Warning Order" came and we were told to prepare several squadrons for deployment to the Middle East. President George H. W. Bush then issued the "Execute Order," ordering warplanes and ground forces to Saudi Arabia after obtaining King Fahd's approval. Iraqi troops had begun to mass along the Saudi border, breaching it at some points, and indicating the possibility that Hussein's forces would continue south into Saudi Arabia's oil fields. Operation DESERT SHIELD, the U.S. military deployment to first defend Saudi Arabia grew rapidly to become the largest American deployment since the Vietnam War. Eventually, 28 nations joined the military coalition arrayed against Iraq, with a further 18 countries supplying economic, humanitarian or other types of assistance.

United States Navy aircraft carriers moved into the Gulf of Oman and the Red Sea, U.S. Air Force interceptors deployed from bases in the United States and airlift transports carried U.S. Army airborne troopers to Saudi Arabia. Navy pre-positioning ships rushed equipment and supplies for an entire Marine brigade from Diego Garcia in the Indian Ocean to the gulf. During the next six months the United States and its Allies built up a powerful force on the Arabian Peninsula. The Navy also began maritime intercept operations in support of a U.S.-led blockade and United Nations sanctions against Iraq.

Marine Aircraft Group 11 was ordered to deploy several

squadrons to Shaikh Isa Air Base in Bahrain. This was a small and very secret air base situated off Saudi Arabia's eastern coast in southern Bahrain. Colonel Rietsch mobilized many of his units, and within a couple of weeks squadrons were flying off to Bahrain to prepare for combat. Several squadrons from MCAS Kaneohe Bay, Hawaii, and MCAS Beaufort, South Carolina, also joined MAG-11 in Bahrain. By September 1990, coalition military units were in place in Saudi Arabia and Bahrain to repel any invasion by Saddam's forces. Although I was involved in the war planning, Colonel Reitsch had me stay back at El Toro to help with any follow on support if needed. Though Luci was relieved and the tenseness in my stomach subsided, deep inside I really wanted to go and put those years of flight training to the ultimate test.

As Desert Shield continued through the fall and early winter of 1990, President Bush grew increasingly impatient with Saddam Hussein. The President had given several warnings to the Iraqi dictator to leave Kuwait or coalition forces, led by U.S. Army General Norman W. Schwartzkoff, would conduct an invasion to liberate Kuwait.

In December 1990, Iraq made a proposal to withdraw from Kuwait provided that their forces were not attacked as they left, and that a consensus was reached regarding the banning of weapons of mass destruction (WMD) in the Palestinian region (Israel). The White House rejected the proposal. Ultimately, the United States maintained its hard-line position that there would be no negotiations until Iraq withdrew from Kuwait and that they should not grant Iraq concessions. They didn't want to give the impression that Iraq benefited from its military campaign. Also, when Secretary of State James Baker met with Saddam's Deputy and Iraqi Foreign Minister, Tariq Aziz, in Geneva for last-minute peace talks in early 1991, Aziz reportedly made no concrete proposals and did not outline any hypothetical Iraqi moves.

I read classified materials every day in early January of 1991. What I read told me it was imminent that the United States would order an invasion of Kuwait and Iraq very soon. On January 16, 1991, my friend, LtCol John "Stuff" Pastuf, came into my office and said "Tora, Tora, Tora," referencing the 1970 war film of the Japanese attack on Pearl Harbor. He just read a top-secret message authorizing coalition forces to launch a massive air campaign, which began the general offensive named Operation Desert Storm. The first priority for coalition forces would be the destruction of the Iraqi Air Force and anti-aircraft facilities. The sorties were launched mostly from Saudi Arabia, Bahrain, as well as from the six aircraft carrier battle groups (CVBG) in the Persian Gulf and Red Sea.

As I flipped on the TV in my office, CNN reported that the invasion had started. President Bush went live to announce to the nation the start of the war and that Iraq would be forced out of Kuwait. At home, my family asked me how long the war would last. I was confident that it would be relatively short. The coalition forces amassed huge armies on the Saudi Arabia/Iraq border, just waiting to move as U.S. air forces hammered Iraqi forces.

About a week into the air campaign, LtCol "Agile" Morrow, the Commanding Officer of MAG-11 Rear, received a call from Col Rietsch directing him to send over more aircraft, specifically the F/A-18D. This was a two-seat version of the Hornet that was used specifically for airborne command and control and as a forward air controller. The officer in the back seat would use the multiple sensors on the aircraft to locate targets for attack, as well as good ol' high-powered binoculars. Once a target was located, the Hornet would swoop down and mark it, using a rocket to explode a cloud of white phosphorous smoke, also known as "Willie Pete." The follow-on attack Hornets, loaded with bombs, would then systematically attack and destroy the marked target. The F/A-18D squadron, VMFA (AW)-121, commanded by Lt Col Steve "Muggo" Mugg, already had six planes in Bahrain flying combat missions. Another six aircraft were needed to be sent to the combat zone.

LtCol Morrow contacted the squadron's Executive Officer, Major Bob "Atlas" Kennedy of VMFA (AW)-121, to prepare the other aircraft for combat. The squadron known as the "Green Knights" immediately had their jets ready to go. However, they were short two pilots. Major Kennedy asked Major "Cheyenne" Bowdie and me to fly two of the six aircraft to the war zone. Inside, I was anxious to get a chance to fly in combat, a feeling I didn't share with my wife.

We were given two days to get ready. A medical team gave us all the vaccines needed in case of a biological attack, and we received the briefings for our flight to Bahrain. I said goodbye to Luci and my children, told them not to worry and that Daddy would be home soon. I must have sounded convincing, at least to my girls, because they assured me that they were not worried.

On January 27, 1991, I was issued my .38 caliber pistol, put on my flight gear and boarded my F/A-18D aircraft. Captain Paul "Pablo" Bless was in the rear seat. My family and several of my neighbors were there to wave us off as our six planes took runways 7L and 7R at MCAS El Toro. We brought our engines to full power, and two by two we roared into the sky. Once I was airborne, I rocked my wings to say goodbye to my family and friends. Looking down I saw them waving along the perimeter road near the end of the runway as we screamed eastward in the skies above them. We stopped at Tinker Air Force Base in Oklahoma City to refuel, and then it was off to MCAS, Beaufort, South Carolina, where we spent the night.

We were awakened at 1:00 a.m. for our briefing to fly the next leg of our mission. We were to fly from South Carolina to the Naval Air Station in Rota, Spain, an 11-hour flight with several aerial refueling points along the way. I wore a rubber body suit under my flight suit in case of problems over the north Atlantic. At that time of year, even with a rubber suit, survivability would be slim in the freezing water. After the briefing, I manned my aircraft in the early morning darkness. A fog layer came over Beaufort, and visibility was less than a quarter of a mile. I slowly taxied my aircraft to the duty runway, and along with the other five aircraft we took off individually with a 10-second delay between aircraft. One by one we rendezvoused above the fog layer, and when all six aircraft were joined up, we were on our way to Europe. We initially flew up the east coast, and then our route would take us just south of Greenland and Iceland, over England, and down into Spain. This way, if anything happened to an aircraft, there would be plenty of airfields along the way to land. Before heading over the open ocean, still dark, we met up with our tanker, an Air Force KC-135, where we positioned three Hornets on each side of the tanker. One by one, at specific points along the route, we would take turns filling up our fuel tanks before continuing on our way, with the KC-135 acting as a pathfinder.

As we flew alongside the tanker the weather grew worse and worse in the darkness. We were flying in storm clouds, visibility was poor and turbulences were rocking the aircraft. When it was time to refuel the third time, the weather was so poor and the turbulences so rough that we were all having problems getting into the fuel basket. If just one aircraft could not get the required fuel, we would all have to divert back to Maine. Finally, all but one of us had refueled when we finally broke into some clear air and out of the storm. The stars sparkled and the air was now smooth as the final Hornet, flown by 1st Lt. Frank "Jason" Richie, with Major Mike "Bake" McBride in the rear seat attempted to take on fuel. Everyone was now at ease as we took some breaths and hoped the worst weather was now behind us.

When Frank went to plug into the tanker, the steel knuckle between the hose and the refueling basket on the KC-135 refueling probe cracked and failed. Fuel began streaming like water through a fire hose down the intakes of Frank's aircraft. Within seconds, both engines caught fire from the intense heat as the fuel ignited in each of the engine compartments. I saw six-foot flames shooting out of both tailpipes, and then I heard Bake cry out on the radio, "Smoke in the cockpit, smoke in the cockpit!"

Both fire-warning lights had illuminated in the front cockpit, and Frank was facing his biggest challenge in his flying career. He reduced both of his engines to idle, broke away from the tanker, and started a descent toward the frigid North Atlantic Ocean. His wingman flew along with him as Frank tried to bring the engines back up to full power, but each time he did the fire lights would come on again. As he continued to drop, one engine showed signs that it may function. The other engine was so badly damaged that he shut it down, so now with just one shaky engine, he began a 300-mile flight to NAS Brunswick, Maine, the closest divert field in the area.

His wingman stayed with him on the flight, while the other four of us diverted to NAS Brunswick, as well. We arrived about an hour earlier than Frank, since we all had two good engines and flew at a much higher altitude. We waited at NAS Brunswick, and then saw in the distance the lights of two aircraft approaching the runway. Crash-and-rescue emergency trucks were waiting as Frank landed his jet and brought it to a stop. When I looked at his aircraft, it was a miracle that he could fly it back, because both engines were disfigured with severe burn damage. That aircraft would not fly again for a couple of years.

Frank would later be awarded the Air Medal for his handling of the situation. The next morning, another aircraft was flown in from MCAS Beaufort to replace the damaged aircraft. That night we took off again and flew successfully to Spain. We then flew from NAS Rota to Shaikh Isa Air Base in Bahrain, an eight-hour flight across the Mediterranean Sea, Egypt and Saudi Arabia. We landed in Bahrain on January 31st, and Colonel Rietsch assigned Major Bowdie and me to the MAG-11 Combat Operations Center (COC), where we went to work for the Air Group's Operations Officer, LtCol John "Player" Cushing. We were beat from our flight but ready for battle.

On February 3, 1991, I briefed for my first combat mission. I was assigned to fly the F/A-18D on a Forward Air Control mission over Kuwait to search for and mark targets. My aircraft was armed with two AIM-9 air-to-air missiles, and two pods of four five-inch Zuni air-to-ground rockets. Captain Reuben "Bone" Padilla was in the rear seat to help me locate targets. He had several combat missions under his belt, so he briefed the flight by reviewing maps of the area and possible targets. We strapped into our aircraft and took off.

Before we entered the combat zone to find targets over Kuwait we refueled on a Marine Corps KC-130 tanker and then we entered enemy airspace. Over Kuwait, we found Iraqi targets, such as artillery pieces, fortified troop embankments and scud missile sites. I successfully marked the first two targets, but on my third run when I rolled in on an artillery site and marked the target for the attack Hornets, I was low when I pulled off target. I heard Bone scream, "BREAK RIGHT, BREAK RIGHT!" He wanted me to pull a maximum G turn to the right to avoid a large surface-to-air missile locked on to us and coming quickly to destroy our aircraft.

I heard him scream louder than I'd ever heard a man scream, "BREAK LEFT!" Again I instinctively pulled hard to the left as another Iraqi surface-to-air missile shot past our left wing. I then gained as much altitude as possible to get out of range of a third missile coming our way. My heart was pumping and the adrenalin flowed as I got my first taste of combat. I thanked Bone for the critical calls that saved my life, but all he said in response was, "Hey, I saved my life, too, up here." Another close call; another life. How many more chances would I get? That was five!! "Hey, Mr. Death, I am now married with children, <u>PLEASE</u> leave me alone," I muttered under my breath.

"What did you say?" inquired Bone.

"Ah, nothing!" I replied.

Later in the war some buddies of mine, F/A-18 pilots Major "Boomer" Knutzen, Major "Cheyenne" Bowdie and Captain "Coma" Quinlan, each were hit by a SAM (surface-to-air). Although they each lost an engine and received significant battle damage, they were able to safely bring their respective aircraft back to Bahrain for a safe landing. Their superb airmanship earned each of them an Air Medal.

I continued to fly multiple combat flights each day, and at nights I worked in the COC. Somewhere in between I found some time to nap. Almost every minute an aircraft was either taking off or landing at Shaikh Isa Air Base. There were rows and rows of bombs, rockets and missiles lined up on the tarmac to load up on the aircrafts. MAG-11 grew to become the largest Marine Fixed Wing Air Group in history, with operational control of all Marine Corps F/A-18A/C/D, A-6E, EA-6B and KC-130F/R/T aircraft in Southwest Asia. Colonel Rietsch quietly told me once, "It's good to be King," as he watched the daily operations of his Air Group from the flight line.

Sometimes threat of death didn't just come while in flight. For example, one night when I was asleep in the barracks, the air raid sirens went off, warning us to put on our gas masks and take cover. In the past couple of weeks there were many false alarms, so I didn't react to this one. Then, suddenly there was a huge explosion, as an Iraqi scud missile landed only a few hundred yards away from the barracks. Not knowing if it contained a chemical or biological warhead, I quickly put on my gas mask and took cover. Two hours later, the all-clear signal was given, and I went back to sleep. It is funny how normal all this becomes. The next morning I walked over to where the missile hit, and there was debris everywhere on the ground, but no one was injured. Just another close call in a war that would be over soon.

The final phase of Desert Storm began early on February 24, 1991, when the Coalition ground offensive began. The objective of the ground war was to expel Iraqi Armed Forces from Kuwait, destroy the Iraqi Republican Guard, and help restore the legitimate government of Kuwait. The plan included a frontal attack along the Kuwait-Saudi Arabia border by the First Marine Expeditionary Force (I MEF) and Arab Coalition Forces (JFC-E and JFC-N) to hold most forward Iraqi divisions in place. Simultaneously, two Army Corps, augmented with French and United Kingdom divisions with more than 200,000 soldiers, would sweep west of the Iraqi defenses deep into Iraq, cut Iraqi lines of communication and destroy the Republican Guard forces. The ground attack went like clockwork and precision. The war was moving rapidly to an end.

On February 26th and 27th, MAG-11 sent aircraft to Highway

80, a six-lane highway between Kuwait and Iraq. The highway runs from Kuwait City to the border town of Safwan and then on to Basra, Iraq. As retreating Iraqi military personnel and others were escaping Kuwait City, MAG-11 and other coalition aircraft destroyed hundreds of vehicles and many of their occupants along the highway. It was actually this scene of devastation on this road, dubbed the Highway of Death that was cited as a factor in President Bush's decision to declare a cessation of hostilities the following day.

I flew down at low level to see the destruction along the highway when I noticed a large open-bed truck weaving in and around the destroyed vehicles at a high speed heading west towards Iraq with about 20 Iraqi soldiers in the back. When they saw me coming their way they began waving their white T-shirts as a sign of surrender. As the rules of engagement state, it would not be ethical in wartime to go ahead and attack the vehicle, but as I flew past the truck I noticed an anti-aircraft gun in the back of the truck shooting at me. Tracer rounds where flying past my canopy. Damn, I thought. Here I was being Mr. Nice guy and they were firing on me, so only equipped with 20 mm rounds in my nose, I reefed my jet around in a hard 270-degree max G turn and with the troops jumping out of the truck as fast as they could. I put the truck in my gun sights and let loose of about 200 rounds as I strafed the truck. Pieces went flying high into the air.

I flew further down the road and came onto several Egyptian

tanks returning from a battle. Several MAG-11 Hornets waiting for a mission at altitude saw them at the same time and asked me to identify them as friend or foe. It was clear they had the mark (a large inverted V) of our coalition partners and I instructed the Hornets they were on our side, but I did locate several artillery pieces that the Iraqis had abandoned and gave the go ahead for the Hornets to unload their bombs on them. This was one of the final missions of the war.

CHAPTER 30

I flew my final combat flight on February 27th and was
able to watch from above the famous tank battle of Medina
Ridge between the United States First Armored Division and
the Second Brigade of the Iraqi Republican Guard Medina
Luminous Division outside Basra. The battle, which waged
for more than two hours, was the largest tank battle of the
war and the largest tank battle in United States history. The
American tanks destroyed 186 Iraqi tanks, and the U.S. lost
none.

As I flew back to Bahrain over the Persian Gulf after my final
combat mission, I noticed that the big guns on the battleships
USS Wisconsin (BB 64) and USS Missouri (BB 63) were quiet
after weeks of constant firepower from their 16-inch guns and
Tomahawk cruise missiles. This was their final battle. The USS
Wisconsin was decommissioned on September 30, 1991, and
the USS Missouri left service on March 30, 1992.

After my final mission, I landed in Bahrain, but before parking
my aircraft I taxied over to the refueling hot pits to fuel up. I
sat back and relaxed as it takes about fifteen minutes to get the
aircraft full. The troops refueling me were looking up at me

in the cockpit and I wrote on a kneeboard card, "THE WAR IS OVER" and showed them. They all let out a yell and it was high fives all around. Then I taxied and parked my aircraft and walked off the flight line. For the first time since I arrived in Bahrain, all the jet engines were quiet.

The next day, on February 28, 1991, President Bush declared a ceasefire and said that Kuwait had been liberated. I had completed 48 combat missions and flew more than 105 combat flight hours in the prior 25 days, earning the same Air Medal that my dad was awarded 47 years earlier. Desert Storm was now over. I was relieved.

I walked to my barracks, laid in bed and slept for over 20 hours straight. I enjoyed the peace and quiet, and when I woke up I was relieved to realize that I had survived the war. Once the official surrender documents were signed, and the war was officially over, it was time to prepare the air group for retrograde back to the United States. Since I was one of the last to arrive I would be one of the last to go home. My job was now to schedule the squadrons to get back to American soil. There would be a lot of work to do over the next few months. The amount of gear, weapons, and supplies would take hundreds of cargo flights and shiploads to get home, but slowly the squadrons and gear left the theater.

Before Colonel Rietsch headed for home, he informed LtCol Cushing that he would be taking command of the Black Knights of VMFA-314 when he returned to MCAS El Toro.

Cushing asked me to be his Executive Officer (XO). I was honored to take the new position with the Black Knights. I had earlier received news that I was selected for promotion to Lieutenant Colonel, and combined with the XO news, I couldn't be more thrilled. Another feather!

The Emir of Bahrain, Sheikh Isa bin Salman al-Khalifa, sent an invitation to Colonel Rietsch and the MAG-11's Executive Officer, Colonel Don "Buff" Beaufait to attend a victory dinner and gathering at his palace in Manama, the capital of Bahrain. Neither of them was interested in attending, so they told me and another officer to attend the function in their place. The invitation indicated the dress would be formal. I obviously had no formal dress attire to wear at the function, so Colonel Rietsch told me to just wear my flight suit and take a military jeep. He said the Emir would understand.

As we pulled up to the palace in our jeep, the guards checked our papers and let us into the large circular red brick driveway where we parked our jeep alongside the many beautifully polished black Mercedes-Benz vehicles and BMWs. As we entered the palace doors, His Highness and his wife, Shaikha Hessa, as well as their twelve children – six sons and six daughters – greeted us as heroes. When we apologized for our dress, the Emir said, "I understand. You came to fight a war, not attend a lavish party."

In attendance at the party was Vice Admiral Stan Arthur, USN, commander of the United States Seventh Fleet and

Commander, U.S. Naval Forces Central Command during Operation Desert Storm. He was in his full military dress uniform, and pulled me aside concerning my dress. I informed him this was all I had to wear and I told him the Emir was fine with me being in a flight suit. Although visibly upset, he didn't pursue the issue any further. I had a few drinks and mingled, talking with ambassadors, sheiks, princes and princesses. My eyes took in the scenery. Everything seemed plated in gold, lavish and extravagant. I'd never seen anything quite like this palace. I tried not to stare.

For dinner, we all gathered around a long table and had a feast of delicacies, the likes of which I'd never seen before or since. Muhammar, which is sweet rice served with dates and sugar was the appetizer. A traditional dish of machboos, consisting of meat and fish served with rice was the first course followed by falafel, fried balls of chickpeas served in a bread, and shawarma, lamb carved from a rotating spit and wrapped in pita bread was the main dish. I wasn't even sure what some of the foods on that table were, but it was truly hard not to stare at it.

After dinner we went into a large ballroom where we were entertained by exquisite dancers and musical arrangements. I felt like Lawrence of Arabia, sitting on large fluffy pillows while watching the night's entertainment. The Emir's oldest son took me upstairs and onto a balcony where we shared a private conversation over a drink. He thanked me for all the

United States did to save Bahrain from Saddam Hussein and his army. That was a proud moment in my life. I returned to the base early in the morning and went right to work. I relayed the evening's events to Colonel Rietsch, and passed on the Emir's best wishes for a job well done by MAG-11.

Throughout my time overseas our troops received thousands of letters from well-wishing Americans. Their letters supported our efforts 100% and helped increase morale. Besides letters we received care packages of food, candy, books, magazines and just about anything we could possibly need. I made many friends through the letter campaign. One night I opened a package from a nice lady from Connecticut and it was full of magazines, soap, toothpaste and mouthwash. After brushing my teeth one evening I took a swig from the mouthwash. It wasn't mouthwash at all. It was bourbon! Alcohol was forbidden on the base, but this was a clever way for her to say thank you to the troops. Several of us had fun passing around the "mouthwash."

One note I need to mention is that as the Iraqi forces were high tailing it back to their border when the end of the war was imminent, they used explosives to blow up hundreds of Kuwaiti oil wells. For weeks after, dense black smoke bellowed from the damaged wells, and a thick dark cloud hung over the Persian Gulf region. Some days when the winds were blowing south, it was impossible to go outside because of the unhealthy air.

One afternoon I was able to get a ride in the back of a helicopter to survey the burning oil wells and see the destruction the Iraqi forces endured during the air and ground war. Hundreds of Iraqi tanks, personnel carriers, artillery pieces, and missile sites were destroyed and lay in ruin in the sand. The blowing sand was slowly burying the hulks that would never see battle again. At Kuwait International Airport three British Airways airliners sat destroyed on the flight line from air strikes. U.S. forces wanted to be sure the Iraqis wouldn't use the aircraft to leave the area. The amount of destruction I observed was just incredible, but the final result was a free Kuwait. Mission accomplished!!! Now time to go home.

It took over two months to retrograde all of MAG-11's aircraft and equipment back to the United States. I flew one of the last F/A-18Ds to leave Bahrain, with Major Mike "Bake" McBride in the rear seat. Colonel Beaufait led the final twelve hornets back home. After stops at NAS Roda, Spain, MCAS Beaufort, South Carolina, Tinker AFB in Oklahoma City, Oklahoma, and MCAS Yuma, Arizona, twelve beautiful Hornets streaked across the sky over MCAS El Toro, on May 17, 1991. One by one we landed our aircraft and then taxied to the flight line where our loved ones stood waiting. I shut down the engines and leaped out of the cockpit. My girls, Kristen and Kathy, and Mike and Luci ran to greet me with all the hugs and kisses I could handle. It was so good to be home.

When I drove home with my family I noticed the beautiful

trees, colorful flower gardens, and the manicured green yards in my neighborhood. This was a far cry from the sand, dust, and barren wastelands of the Middle East. My neighbors honked their horns and waved as I drove up to my house. A large banner stretched across the garage doors, saying, "Welcome Home, Major DAD." That night I slept in my own bed with my wife. It felt as if I had been gone a lifetime.

The following weekend we had a huge block party celebrating the success of the war, and my return home to the neighborhood. It was reassuring to have such nice neighbors and friends, and to learn that they had been kind to my family when I was off at war. With this grand reception I pondered how poorly our Vietnam veterans were received when they came home from combat. America had come a long way. A neighbor who served in Vietnam was in tears when he came up and hugged me. "Now this is the way American troops should be welcomed home," he said. "God bless you, Greg, and thank you."

CHAPTER 31

On May 27, 1991, LtCol Cushing took command of VMFA-314, a single seat F/A-18 squadron, and I assumed the Executive Officer position. At the squadron there were many personnel changes, promotions and awards that I arranged and managed in my new position. In mid-June we deployed for two weeks to the Air Force Air Defense Military Exercise, code name Cope Thunder, at Elmendorf Air Force Base, in Anchorage, Alaska. The exercise consisted of ten days of very realistic air combat training that gave me a chance to observe the skills of the squadron pilots. I observed and evaluated their flight planning and mission execution. Most of the Black Knights were combat veterans and performed extremely well.

It was great to be in a squadron again, flying and training in the F/A-18 Hornet. Luci and the children were off for summer break, and they enjoyed the southern California lifestyle. Laguna Beach was their favorite place to go for fun in the sun. In the summer, relatives from Phoenix would visit to get out of the Arizona heat and we would join them at the beaches. It was always nice to play a volleyball game in the sand or a pick-up basketball game on the courts at Laguna Beach. Mike and the twins loved to body surf on the large waves that occasionally pounded the beach.

At the squadron I was busy keeping up to speed in the aircraft. I left for a weekend of cross-country training in late July that took me to Colorado, Florida, Ohio and Nebraska. I didn't know that I was about to use up yet another life... or that I'd be given another chance.

During one of the legs of my flight, as I had just taken off out of Cleveland International Airport, a huge flock of large birds flew in front of me. I tried to avoid them, but hit several of the large creatures, feathers flying. I'd heard about this sort of thing, but never experienced it. I held my breath as some of the birds went down the engine intakes of my aircraft that started to sputter and cough. I heard loud compression stalls coming from both engines. I declared an emergency and returned safely back to Cleveland after dumping some fuel to get to landing weight.

As I pulled up to the ramp, I shut the engines down, got out of the craft and assessed the damage. Both engines were destroyed and coated with blood, guts, and feathers. The engines weren't the only parts of the craft that were ravaged. The birds struck both of my wings, the tail, the windscreen and the landing gear. This was a mess because the birds were stuck in the nose landing gear compartment as it was retracting into the body of the plane just as I had taken off. I estimated that more than 20 birds hit the aircraft. PETA would not have been happy with me. I had just dodged another potentially fatal accident. A cargo plane brought out two new engines with a maintenance crew, and within a couple of days I was back home. Man, I started thinking that I might be running out of lives. If the old adage is true about nine lives, I only had three to go! I'd have to be careful.

In November 1991, my commanding officer went through a tragedy no parent would ever want to face, something so horrific that it's difficult to put down on paper now. His wife had been taking anti-anxiety medication for some time. It had begun to affect her behavior. They were having marital problems, but nothing serious. My CO needed a break from work and left for a fishing trip, leaving his wife with their two young girls, ages four and eight. That evening his wife brought their two young girls into her bed and shot them with a .38 caliber handgun. Then she turned the gun on herself. A shot to the head for each of them, but her plan for a family suicide went awry. She killed her children, but she survived her own head wound. She was later acquitted for the killings for reason of insanity and would be institutionalized in a psychiatric hospital where she would remain for several years.

I received a call from LtCol Pastuf who shared the grim news with me, and I rushed to their house, where I found the fall out. It was an incredibly disturbing scene, but I wanted to be there when my boss came home. Someone needed to take the helm in his absence. The police and coroner were there; we frantically contacted him to tell him to come home. When we finally reached him, he rushed home, but upon entering his home to see the devastation he collapsed. There was no comforting him. We were all in disbelief. Why was life so difficult at times? A senseless act like this affected so many people; I just couldn't get a grip on such behavior.

He was in no position emotionally to command a squadron or fly an aircraft, and he was relieved of his duties. LtCol Ron "Shark" Richards was brought in to take over command. It was a sad time for all of us in the squadron. My former boss needed a lot of time to heal, and he would eventually go back to flying and command another squadron.

I looked to 1992 to be a better, less stressful year. Shark kept me on as his Executive Officer and brought in several new members for his team. We made a few small deployments, but for the most part we stayed at El Toro and flew in the local training areas against local squadrons. Then, in May 1992, Shark and I were summoned to Colonel Beaufait's office for a meeting. Beaufait informed us that our squadron would be attached to the Navy's Carrier Air Wing Eleven (CVW-11) on the aircraft carrier USS Abraham Lincoln (CVN-72).

The Navy was short a squadron and came to the Marine Corps to fill the void. Shark was not pleased with this news, and I was in no mood to go back to sea. Our carrier cruise was scheduled for June 1993. This would give us just over a year to get prepared for aircraft carrier duty. All the pilots had to qualify on the carrier and stay proficient. The maintenance personnel would have to learn about life at sea on a carrier.

The next 14 months would be intense training for us with CVW-11, which would include training at the Naval Air Station, in Fallon, Nevada, and two- to three-week cruises on the USS Abraham Lincoln. The cruise in June 1993 would be for six months and would take me back to the Persian Gulf to fly combat flights over Southern Iraq to enforce the no-fly zone. Since the end of Desert Storm, Saddam was up to his old tricks again, and we were directed to stop his military aircraft from flying below the 32nd parallel.

In August 1992, it was time to get back up to speed with my aircraft carrier landings. All of us pilots practiced our landings for about a month at El Toro, and then we went out to sea and got our required 10 day landings, and six night landings. This time we landed on the aircraft carrier USS Eisenhower (CVN-69) that was just off the coast of San Diego. Once we were all qualified again, we joined CVW-11 and came under operational control of the Navy.

The Carrier Air Group Commander (CAG) was Navy Captain Daniel "Gabby" Gabriel, who welcomed us into his air wing. We trained hard with the wing, flying almost every day and learning the various missions required for large penetrating air strikes from an aircraft carrier. This would be interesting.

In September 1992, Luci transferred to Mission San Juan Capistrano Catholic School where she taught sixth grade. As a Catholic I found its history intriguing. The Mission was founded by the Spanish Catholics of the Franciscan Order in

1775 by Father Lasuen, though all school-aged children will tell you that it was Father Serra's work that is remembered. They learn about him in about fifth grade, devoting a lot of time to building missions out of sugar cubes and drawing maps of early California.

Aside from being a beautiful part of our country, San Juan Capistrano has the distinction of being home to the oldest building in California still in use, a chapel built in 1782. Tradition has it that cliff swallows arrive at the Mission on March 19, Saint Joseph's Day, and fly south on Saint John's Day, October 23. The cliff swallow is a migratory bird that spends its winters in Argentina but makes the 6,000-mile flight north to the warmer climes of the American southwest in springtime.

Kristen and Kathy would transfer to the Mission School where they entered third grade. Mike was a sophomore at Santa Margarita Catholic High School by this point, excelling in football and baseball. He did really well in academics, too, which made my heart swell. I was proud of our little family. They supported me in everything I did professionally, even when it meant they had to move several times. Through it all I was thankful to have Luci be the strong mother she was to keep everything together. I look back on those years now with utter amazement.

With the family doing well and my training on track, the Black Knights deployed to NAS Fallon, Nevada, for five weeks of training with CAG-11. We trained for all sorts of scenarios. During one mission, I flew wing for Captain John "Scorch" Daly, a young officer with incredible talent in our squadron. We went up against a couple of the Top Guns who were flying the F-5 aircraft. The mission was 2v2, meaning two of us and two of them. We took about 30 miles in separation and then headed toward each other. The objective? To shoot them down before they shot us down (simulated, of course).

Everything was going well until I lost sight of Scorch and my air-to-air TACAN (the indicator that shows how far apart we were) showed Scorch was 1.2 miles away from my craft. That was the required distance for this particular engagement. I radioed Scorch to let him know that I had lost sight of him, but we continued our attack. I then noticed .8 on the indicator as I continued to look for Scorch and he for me, then .4, then .3, then .2, then .1 as my head was on a swivel, knowing he was very close. The hair on the back of my neck was standing up when I heard a loud thump under me as Scorch passed within a few feet of my aircraft; neither one of us saw the other. Luckily, we missed each other, I regained sight, and we continued our pursuit down range to kill the F-5s. That was too close for comfort! The way I saw it, I must have had an angel on my shoulder. Two more lives to go.

We finished the training at NAS Fallon just before Christmas and returned home to MCAS El Toro for the holidays. After that, it was off to the aircraft carrier for three weeks of training. When spring came, we were just three months from deployment to the Persian Gulf. Shark received word that he had been selected for the rank of Colonel. This put him taking the squadron on the cruise in jeopardy, since typically a squadron Commanding Officer is the rank of Lieutenant Colonel. The new MAG-11 CO, Colonel George "Cajun" Tullus, informed Shark that he would be reassigned to take command of the F/A-18 replacement pilot training squadron, VMFAT-101, a large squadron that was commanded by a Colonel. With his reassignment, I was elevated to the position of Squadron CO at a change of command ceremony on our flight line. That's a day that will be forever in my memory: April 9, 1993.

Another date would be cemented in my mind that year, not too long after the ceremony. On May 5, 1993, my beloved Aunt Rita died after a long struggle with cancer. Aunt Rita and I shared a special bond. She was one of my greatest cheerleaders throughout my life. Her love and support gave me more strength to pursue my dreams. I still miss my Aunt Rita to this day. God rest her soul.

CHAPTER 32

As Commanding Officer of a Marine Fighter/Attack Squadron, I had 18 pilots, 225 enlisted maintenance and support personnel, and ten aircraft. It was now my job to take the squadron to sea to the Persian Gulf. The maintenance crews worked 24 hours a day getting the jets ready for sea duty and did a masterful job. On June 15, 1993, the USS Abraham Lincoln departed its home port at Alameda, California. I said my goodbyes to my family and friends, and that night my squadron flew aboard the aircraft carrier, completely focused on the unique challenge ahead. Our mission was to enforce the United Nations (UN) Resolution Number 688, that is, to ensure no Iraqi military aircraft was to fly south of the 32nd parallel over Iraq. This operation was code named, Operation Southern Watch. Before we entered the Persian Gulf, we made two port visits, a short stop in Hawaii, to load up with some weapons and jet fuel, and a five-day visit to Hong Kong.

Luci flew to Hong Kong to meet me for a short vacation. A couple of the other officer's wives also came, and we all had a great time. Hong Kong, situated on China's south coast, is renowned for its expansive skyline and deep natural harbor. With a landmass of only 426 square miles and a population of seven million people, Hong Kong is one of the most densely populated areas in the world. We took in the sights and ate some wonderful meals, but the time was ticking when I would have to say my goodbyes again, and this time for five and a half months.

After our port visit to Hong Kong, it was all business as we sailed the Indian Ocean toward the Persian Gulf. On the evening of July 20, 1993, during a night approach to the carrier, an F-14 Tomcat got very low during the approach and crashed into the back of the ship. Aircraft debris and fire lit up the carrier deck and the aircraft was destroyed. The pilot was killed, but the officer in the rear seat survived after he ejected from the cockpit. A helicopter from the ship picked him up at sea. This was a horrific accident, but within a half hour, after the fire was extinguished and aircraft parts were cleaned up, the ship was landing aircraft again. This was a testimony to the professionalism of the ship's crewmembers and squadron personnel to handle emergencies. I had three young rookies flying that night and they did a stellar job conserving fuel and remaining calm until the Lincoln was ready to land aircraft. One by one they landed with minimum fuel in their tanks, but safe they were as they shut down their engines and came below deck. I gave each a bear hug and was glad they were safe. One of my pilots landed with zero fuel registered on his fuel gauge. If the flight deck would not have been cleared in time to land the aircraft, the plan was to have all the pilots eject and be picked up by the ship's helicopters. That would not have been good just one month into the cruise. Sadly, we buried the Tomcat pilot at sea after a solemn ceremony on the hangar deck.

On July 24th, we entered the Persian Gulf through the narrow passage, called the Straits of Hormuz. With Iran to our east, and Saudi Arabia to our west, we flew strategic missions over Iraq through Saudi airspace. We flew in flights of two, armed with air-to-air missiles, and high-speed anti-radiation missiles (HARM). The HARM is used to detect and lock-on at range to hostile ground radar emissions. Our missions became routine after a while. The Iraqi air force would never enter the no-fly zone, some came close, but turned around at the last moment. Another squadron aircraft from our air wing did shoot a couple of HARM missiles at Iraqi ground radars that locked on to them. Other than that incident, the operation went smooth.

One night when I was catapulted from the aircraft carrier I forgot to pressurize my cockpit. As I climbed to altitude, I took off my oxygen mask for comfort's sake (against regulations), and as I reached thirty thousand feet I began to feel groggy and tired. I looked at my pressure altitude gauge that should have been reading about eight thousand feet and it showed thirty thousand feet. I was within a few seconds of passing out from oxygen starvation, so I grabbed my oxygen mask and put it on, taking in 100% oxygen. Within a couple of minutes I was feeling better. That could have been a fatal mistake on my part. Being a seasoned aviator I should have known better, but I did recognize the symptoms of oxygen starvation, and reacted correctly. I was now down to my last life, and since I am writing this book I obviously never used it.

On September 10, 1993, we had a five-day port visit in Jebel Ali, United Arab Emirates. I celebrated my 40th birthday at the Chicago Beach Hotel on the Persian Gulf. The officers from my squadron threw a birthday barbeque for me on the beach with an authentic Arabian belly dancer putting on a show. It was good to be off the ship to spend some time relaxing away from the stresses of the ship and carrier flying.

In late September 1993, we were preparing to leave the Persian Gulf for home, but on October 3rd Task Force Ranger of the U.S. Special Operations Forces, operating in Somalia, attempted to capture the Somalia self-proclaimed President Mohammad Aidid, and his foreign minister, Omar Elmi. Two U.S. Army Black Hawk helicopters were shot down during the raid, and a surviving pilot, Chief Warrant Officer Mike Durant was taken hostage. Overall, eighteen U.S. personnel died and seventy-eight were wounded, along with over one thousand Somali casualties. The USS Abraham Lincoln was directed by the National Command Authority to head to the Somalia coast to provide fixed wing air cover. Within 96 hours, at high speeds that are classified but eye watering, the USS Abraham

Lincoln was on station off the Somalia coast. We stayed off the coast and flew missions over the capital city of Mogadishu for several weeks. Finally, on November 3, 1993, we left the Somalia coast for home.

On November 12, 1993, we stopped in Perth, Australia for a port visit for some well-deserved rest and relaxation. Again, the people of Australia were very kind and friendly to us. The U.S. Ambassador to Australia threw a big party for the ship's officers. Admiral Joseph J. Dantone, Jr., Commander of Carrier Group Three, Captain Richard J. Nibe, Commanding Officer of the USS Abraham Lincoln, and our new CAG, Captain James D. MacAurthur, Jr., were the honored guests. It was a gala event for all of us. We had a huge feast with plenty of drinks, an evening we all needed after such a long period at sea.

I received a message from my headquarters that my squadron was given a quota for one of my pilots to attend the prestigious Navy Fighter Weapons School, also known as Top Gun, in Fightertown USA, NAS Miramar, California. This was one school every fighter pilot in the Navy and Marine Corps wanted to attend, and with the 1986 release of the movie, Top Gun, starring Tom Cruise, Val Kilmer and Kelly McGillis, it was even more sought after by the "best of the best." I sat down with my senior staff and we selected Scorch Daly to fill our quota, and just like in the movie I summoned him to my stateroom to give him the news. Unaware why I wanted to see him he came into my office and came to attention as I told him,

"I am giving you your dream shot. You are going to be flying with the best of the best. You are going to Top Gun when we get back home."

Relieved to know he wasn't in trouble he exhaled and with a big smile he said, "Thank you, Sir," before leaving my stateroom. It was a good feeling to award my best pilots.

From Perth, we transited the Celebes Sea, then through the Balabac and Surigao Straits, and on November 23, 1993 we celebrated Thanksgiving onboard the carrier. The ship cooks prepared turkey with all the trimmings for us. On December 5th we stopped at Pearl Harbor, Hawaii to unload some weapons and we picked up our "Tigers." Tigers are civilian relatives of shipboard members who would then sail with us from Hawaii to California. From December 8th to the 14th, they could observe carrier operations. My son, Mike, flew to Hawaii and sailed with me for that week at sea. He was 17 years old and had a great time, and I enjoyed showing him what I did at sea.

Before our aircraft flew off the ship on December 14th to El Toro, all the squadron pilots met below deck for an awards ceremony. Each carrier landing is graded by the Landing Signal Officer. At the end of a carrier cruise, all the grades are compiled, and our 114 carrier pilots are rated in linear order. Of a possible 4.0 perfect score, I received a 3.81, and a 100% boarding rate, which put me on the top of all the pilots, earning me the "Top Hook Award." This achievement was my proudest accomplishment as an aviator, bar none. Admiral Dantone and Captain MacAurthur both congratulated me for a job well done, especially for a Marine Corps pilot. Three other of my pilots made it into the Top 10, Captain David "Crusoe" Robinson, Major Jim "Skull" Brownlowe, and Captain Dave "Lepp" Leppelmeier. My squadron was the first Marine Corps squadron in six years to cruise with a Navy air wing and the squadron performed flawlessly. The enlisted maintenance crews and administrative support troops did an awesome job and made me proud. It was a team effort!!

On the afternoon of December 14th, 10 aircraft from the Black Knights flew off the carrier and landed at MCAS El Toro, California. I led the flight to the airfield and we all landed in order. When I pulled up to the tarmac, Luci, Kristen and Kathy were there to welcome me home. It was a great homecoming, but these long absences from family were getting old.

On January 14, 1994, I received a phone call from my brother, Bob, who informed me that my Uncle Bob, Rita's husband, had a fatal heart attack in Tempe, Arizona. He had just finished jogging with my oldest sister, Jean, when he collapsed and died. It was so sad, especially for Jim, Marie, and Peggy, who only the previous year lost their mother. Luci and I went back to Phoenix for the funeral and to help comfort my cousins.

When I returned to California after the funeral I transitioned the Black Knights back to a land-based squadron at MCAS

El Toro. I commanded the squadron for another year, and on November 18, 1994, I gave command to Lieutenant Colonel "Yogi" Hughes at a Change of Command ceremony on the flight line. It was hard for me to leave the Black Knights after all we had been through, but my time was up. In 1994, I was awarded the Tactical Pilot Achievement Award from the Association of Naval Aviation (ANA), and the Pilot of the Year Award from Marine Forces Pacific. My squadron won the Chief of Naval Operations Safety Award (CNO), and the Fleet Marine Forces Pacific Fighter/Attack Squadron of the Year Award. My maintenance officer, Captain Dave Kelly, received an award for his work aboard ship supervising the maintenance department. Several of the enlisted men received commendation and achievement medals for their hard work. I was so proud of my men!

I was now coming to the 20-year mark of my military service. It is at this juncture that military personnel ponder retiring from military service. Many pilots leave the service to fly with the commercial airlines, but after discussion with Luci, I decided to stay in the service a while longer. I was selected to attend the National Defense University in Washington, D.C. to pursue a Master's Degree in National Resource Strategy. With this assignment, it meant another move across the country. With the twins now twelve years old, I knew that they would not take the news very well. They had all their friends at school and in the neighborhood and they were not looking to start all over again.

Mike was at the University of Arizona in Tucson pursuing a degree in Criminal Justice and he was not concerned where we lived. He was a member of the Navy ROTC Program and had his goal set to be a military aviator. In fact, in May 1995, I took Mike up for a ride in the F/A-18D. As a member of ROTC, he received authorization to fly in a military aircraft. We took off from MCAS El Toro and flew a training mission over the Pacific Ocean with two other Hornets. We had a great time in the air together and it was after that flight that he really had his goal set on becoming a military aviator.

As we packed up again for another move, Kristen and Kathy took it really hard. They said their goodbyes to their friends and cried as we drove away from our neighborhood. I was able to rent my house to a friend and I had already rented a nice home for us in Fairfax, Virginia. After the cross-country road trip we pulled up to our new home in Fairfax as the moving company was there waiting for us to unload our household goods. The twins met a nice neighbor girl, Kara Schlifke, which made things a little easier for them. They enrolled at Robinson Middle School in Fairfax for the 7th grade. Luci found a job teaching the 5th grade at Cunningham Park Elementary School in Vienna, Virginia, and I prepared for my next educational experience.

I began my studies in August 1995 at the National Defense University located at Fort McNair, Washington, D.C. The curriculum focused on how to resource the national military strategy, from building airplanes to tanks. It was a very interesting course. In the spring of 1996 our class went to Europe for three weeks to see how the Europeans approached their national strategy. We visited Germany, France, Denmark, Finland, Switzerland and Italy. The trip opened my eyes to the various economic heavyweights in Western Europe. I enjoyed mingling with the people of these countries and hear how they enjoyed life in Europe.

When I had a weekend off, I went to Nice and Monte Carlo on the French Rivera. Located on the southeast coast of France on the Mediterranean Sea, Nice is the second-largest French city on the Mediterranean coast after Marseille. The spectacular natural beauty of the Nice area and its mild Mediterranean climate made me want to live here permanently. But the beauty of Monte Carlo was second to none. Near the western end of the city is the world-famous Place du Casino, the gambling center that has made Monte Carlo an international playground for the wealthy. Large yachts are harbored in the bay as their crews wash and wax them as they wait for their owners to move on to another Mediterranean port. Monte Carlo is the home of the famous Monaco Grand Prix, a Formula One motor race held each year on the Circuit de Monaco. The race was scheduled for the following weekend and several of the drivers were practicing on the circuit. As an avid race fan, this was a sight to see as the noisy machines wove their way around the tight course. It was hard for me to leave this area and head home to the United States.

Graduation was set for June 12, 1996, but before I graduated, my monitor, Major "Bone" Padilla, looked for a follow up job for me in the Washington, D.C. area. There were various jobs available at the Pentagon for a Lieutenant Colonel, but he found an opening at the White House Military Office (WHMO) as Assistant Chief of Staff. I was sent to the White House to interview for the position. There were eight of us that were interviewed by the Honorable Alan P. Sullivan, Deputy Assistant to the President and Director of the White House Military Office. After the first day of interviews I was a finalist for the position, and I was called in again for a second interview. This time I interviewed with the Chief of Staff of the White House Military Office, Colonel James A. Hawkins, USAF. That evening I received a phone call telling me I was selected for this very prestigious position.

The White House Military Office is located in the East Wing of the White House. Besides the Director, Chief of Staff, and my position, there were six of us that worked in the office. I was overwhelmed with my selection. At age 42, I would be working at the highest level in government. President Clinton was concluding his first term as President when I arrived in July 1996. My position would be for three years. Luci and the children were thrilled to hear the news. The twins were ready to start the 8th grade and they had met a lot of new friends, so three more years in Fairfax was okay with everyone.

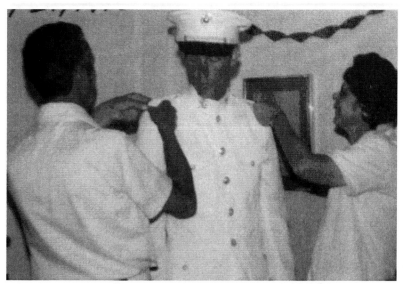

My Second Lieutenant Commissioning Ceremony.
My parents pinning on my gold bars.
May 1975 in Phoenix, Arizona.

My best friend, Nick Ganem, at my
Commissioning Ceremony. May, 1975.

My roommate, Dave Rann, and me at
The Basic School, Quantico, Virginia, 1975.

At the Rifle Range with my M-16 Rifle,
The Basic School, Quantico, Virginia, 1976.

Ready to start flying. In front of my T-34B
Mentor. Saufley Field, Pensacola, Florida, 1976.

My flight instructor, Navy Lt. Klint with me in front of the
T-2C Buckeye, Meridian, Mississippi, 1976.

My cousins, Peggy, Jim and Marie Jorgensen.
Alhambra High School Football, Phoenix, Arizona, 1976.

On a cross-country flight at Williams AFB, Arizona, in my
T/A-4 Skyhawk with my Aunt Rita, and cousins,
Peggy, and Marie.

Luci and me on our Wedding Day, St. Gregory's Church,
Phoenix, Arizona, March 6, 1982.

Luci's sister, Linda Farrell, Luci and our twin girls, Kristen
and Kathryn, Grandpa and Grandma Fanelli, and Luci's
brother, Sam, Jeanette, Pennsylvania, 1983.

My family: Me, Kathy, Mike, Kristen and Luci,
Clinton Township, Michigan, 1987.

On an Aircraft Carrier as Landing Signal Officers (LSOs),
Chuck "Overstress" Strong and me.

RF-4B Phantom II landing aboard the USS Midway.

My F/A-18D aircraft during Operation Desert Storm,
Shaikh Isa Air Base, Bahrain, 1991.

On duty at the Combat Operation Center (COC)
with Marine Aircraft Group 11, Bahrain, 1991.

F/A-18A with battle damage to the engines during
Desert Storm. Flown by Major "Boomer" Knutzen, 1991.

F/A-18A Hornet from VMFA-314, The Black Knights, dropping bombs and letting out flares. Desert Storm, 1991.

My girls, Kristen and Kathy, welcoming me home from Desert Storm, MCAS El Toro, California, May, 1991.

Commanding Officer of VMFA-314, The Black Knights
onboard the USS Abraham Lincoln, 1993-1994.

F/A-18A Hornet landing aboard the
USS Abraham Lincoln in the Indian Ocean, 1993.

SECTION THREE

YEARS AT THE WHITE HOUSE

During my time in the military as a fighter pilot I had defied
death on more than one occasion. These events would help
strengthen me for my new life at the White House, where I'd
be called upon to make decisions to ensure our Commander-
in-Chief had what he needed to effectively discharge his office.
These were more difficult times than many Americans knew.

CHAPTER 33

It took almost a month for me to receive all the special clearances necessary to work at the White House. Background checks into my character, finances and education, as well as fingerprinting and polygraph testing were all completed before I could receive my credentials (called a Yankee White clearance) that would allow me to come and go onto the White House grounds. I was assigned an office in the East Wing, issued a parking spot and received a diplomatic passport. This was to me like something out of the movies! However, I didn't let anyone at the White House know just how thrilled I was to be allowed to work there. Maybe all the staff felt the same. After all, it isn't something that everyone gets to do in life.

Over my first two weeks at the White House I received thorough briefings by the military units that come under the White House Military Office responsibility. The officer I was to replace, Lt. Col. Larry Spenser, USAF, took me around to all the military units that our office supervised. I first visited Andrews Air Force Base in Prince George County, Maryland, where our President's airplanes are maintained, two Boeing 747-200Bs and several other military aircraft for Presidential airlift use. Each is adapted to meet our President's unique needs and to make him safe and comfortable during flight. The name Air Force One does not belong to any specific aircraft, but instead is a radio call sign used when the President is onboard any United States Air Force plane. To allow the President to fulfill his duties as Commander-in-Chief, the aircraft have state-of-the-art communications equipment onboard.

At that time, the Air Force One squadron was commanded by Colonel Robert D. "Danny" Barr, USAF. The 4,000 square feet of floor space inside Air Force One includes a Presidential stateroom, an executive dressing room and shower, a conference room, a dining room, two fully equipped kitchens, a Presidential office, a medical treatment room, secretarial offices and six lavatories. It's like a classy condo with wings.

The aircraft is broken down into four areas. The front of the aircraft is where the President travels, next is the seating for White House Staff, then there is the area for Presidential guests, and in the back of the plane is where the White House Press Corps travels. The protocol onboard Air Force One is that passengers are never allowed to move forward into another area without permission. That's why members of the press are seated in the rear of the airplane and are never allowed out of their section. In the upper deck of the 747 is where several Air Force radio operators perform their duties, keeping the President connected with the world. The cockpit is manned by the best pilots in the Air Force, each screened, evaluated and trained extensively to perform the duties as a

Presidential pilot.

My next brief was in Quantico, Virginia, home of HMX-1, which is the Presidential helicopter squadron that was at the time commanded by Colonel Frederick J. Geier, USMC. Like Air Force One, Marine One is a radio call sign used when the President is aboard a Marine Corps helicopter. The Sikorsky VH-3D, a special helicopter designed for Presidential flights, is the most used, because it is a versatile and reliable means of transportation for the Commander-in-Chief at a moment's notice. It is usually used to fly the President to and from Andrews Air Force Base from the South Lawn of the White House. HMX-1 has a fleet of helicopters to provide the President and Vice President, as well as cabinet members and foreign dignitaries, with helicopter lifts throughout the world.

Located 70 miles from the White House in the Catoctin Mountains near Thurmont, Maryland, is a Presidential retreat named Camp David. Established in 1942 as a place for the President to relax and entertain, Camp David is known to most Americans. They've probably heard about it at some point in their lives, so it's not exactly a secret spot, but it is a beautiful getaway.

President Franklin Delano Roosevelt wanted to escape the summer heat of Washington, D.C., so he went to the higher altitude of Camp David to enjoy its cool breezes and good security. I was flown there in a helicopter and received a briefing on the operations of the camp. The name of the camp was originally named "Shangri-La" after the mountain kingdom in James Hilton's book, Lost Horizon. It was renamed Camp David in 1953 by President Eisenhower in honor of his grandson, David. The camp is operated by Navy personnel, and when I was there Commander Bert Ramsay, USN, was in charge. The Chaplin for the retreat was a Navy Lieutenant, and when I met him we both grew big smiles. He was the Chaplin for MAG-11 during Desert Storm and we both hugged and reminisced about our days in Bahrain during the war. It was so nice to see a friendly face. During my tour at the White House I made it a point to get to Camp David on a Sunday to listen to one of his sermons.

Marines from the barracks in Washington, D.C., provide permanent security for Camp David. Guests at Camp David can enjoy a pool, a putting green, three-hole golf course, tennis courts, a private bowling alley, gymnasium and many guest cabins, "Dogwood," "Maple", "Birch" and "Rosebud," to name a few.

The Presidential cabin is named "Aspen Lodge," and as you might expect, it comes brilliantly complete with all the amenities a President could want and is filled with well-made rustic furnishings that reminds one of a high-class ski lodge. From the expansive window in the living room, I looked out over the mountain. The view was breathtaking. The cabin is positioned in such a way as to also look over the pool and golf course, and the whole place is surrounded by gorgeous Aspen trees, strong and tall. I also toured the historic conference room where President Carter brokered peace between Egyptian President Anwar Sadat and Israeli Prime Minister Menachem Begin in 1978, known as the Camp David Peace Accords.

My next briefing was at the Naval Support Facility at Anacostia, Washington, D.C., headquarters for the White House Communications Agency (WHCA), which provides communication systems that enable the President and his staff to lead the nation efficiently. The agency provides worldwide audio-visual, voice and data communications support for the President, Vice President, Presidential emissaries, White House staff, the United States Secret Service and others as directed by the White House Military Office. WHCA supports the President at the White House and in the Washington metropolitan area. In addition, they deploy teams worldwide to support Presidential travel missions. WHCA also sets up and records radio broadcasts for the President from any location around the world, videotapes Presidential movements, processes film from official White House photographers and makes video recordings for the White House and staff. Before I had the grand tour, I had no idea of the extent of the services WHCA provided, and I admit that I was more than a little blown away to be a part of all of the inner workings.

The President has five military officers, also known as military aides, which consists of one officer from each branch of service who works with the Secret Service and the Pentagon to ensure the President's security, particularly when he is out of D.C. These military aides come under the White House Military Office responsibility and are located in an office that was next to mine. I can tell you who they were: Lt. Col. Michael G. Mudd, USA; Commander John M. Richardson, USN; Major Robert Patterson, USAF; Major Charles Raderstorf, USMC; and Lieutenant Commander June. E. Ryan, USCG. Just as the men and women who hold these positions now in today's administration, these officers carried the codes, known as the football, for America's nuclear arsenal, and I assure you that an officer is near the President 24 hours a day.

Every day I was briefed by one organization or another, and I learned the intricacies that made the White House function like a well-oiled machine. Total number of military personnel that provide direct support to the White House is roughly two thousand. Throughout the White House I met the staff and was educated on each of their responsibilities. Our job at the military office was to ensure that the President, Vice President and their staff were met with the highest standards of quality provided to them by the U.S. military. Every day we were involved in one aspect or another with the President's schedule. We were always on alert and at the ready for anything.

The Presidential travel office came under our responsibility when it came to Presidential transportation. Each Presidential flight had to be scheduled and manifested correctly, zero room for error. Whenever the President traveled it had to be determined if it was an official trip, a political trip or a re-election trip. An official trip would not be charged, but if it was a political or re-election trip, the President and his guests would be charged for the trip. A political trip was paid for by the Democratic National Committee, and a re-election trip was paid for by the 1996 Clinton/Gore Reelection Committee. We charged First Class airfare, too. The money would go back into our military account. All press members who fly on Air Force One as part of the press pool were also charged airfare, but they were the worst when it came to settling their accounts. Several news agencies were forbidden to fly until they paid off their debt.

The President's medical team was headed by Captain Eleanor "Connie" Mariano, USN. She was President Clinton's primary care physician, and she had a team of two doctors and six nurses who took care of the President's medical needs. Whenever President Clinton traveled you could be sure that a doctor and two nurses would always travel with him. Dr. Mariano was an extraordinary physician who made President Clinton's health her priority. She would later be promoted to Admiral.

Other parts of the White House are devoted to more personal needs. For example, there's a nice dining room in the West Wing basement staffed by Navy chefs to prepare meals for the White House staff and their guests. Colonel Hawkins took me there for breakfast where I met some of the staff. As I looked around the dining room I noticed several prominent staff members, including Andy Lake and Sandy Berger, the President's National Security Advisor and Deputy National Security Advisor, respectively. These larger-than-life figures were mere mortals as I observed them reading the newspaper, laughing, and sipping their coffee. I looked down and finished my breakfast and felt at ease in their company.

The Director of the Special Contingency Programs Office provided me with classified briefs. In doing so, I was comfortable concerning the safety of the President and White House staff members. I was overwhelmed with the enormous support the White House Military Office provides the President. I recall walking down the colonnade between the White House mansion and the West Wing with the gorgeous Rose Garden off to my left, feeling a sense of reverence, knowing that many American Presidents strolled along the same walkway. Halfway down the colonnade I stopped and looked out over the Rose Garden and took it all in. Multicolored roses surrounded a meticulously groomed lawn where many White House events had taken place. World leaders had shared the lawn with our Presidents announcing treaties, agreements, and taking questions from the press concerning world events. When Bill Clinton was a young man, he shook hands with then President Kennedy, in the Rose Garden.

After all my initial briefings, Colonel Hawkins introduced me to Leon Panetta, White House Chief of Staff; Bruce Lindsey, Deputy White House Counsel; Jodie Torkelson, Assistant to the President for Administration; Mike McCurry, White House Press Secretary; George Stephanopoulous, Senior Advisor for Policy and Strategy; and Debra Schiff, West Wing Receptionist. We then went into the offices of Nancy Hernreich, Director of Oval Office Operations, and Betty Currie, Personal Secretary to the President. After meeting them, they took me into the Oval Office. I felt a sense of awe as I looked around the oval room, but I couldn't show my feelings. I looked around and nodded. Uh, huh… Uh, huh… Like this was a normal day in my life! I walked over and touched President Clinton's desk and looked at his family pictures and military challenge coins displayed behind his desk chair. I couldn't help but smile just a little as I walked on the beautiful deep blue rug with the Presidential seal woven in the center. Two red and white candy striped sofas were placed facing each other along with two gold chairs for the President and his guests. Overlooking the room was a portrait of our first President, George Washington. Was this really happening?

CHAPTER 34

The Oval Office radiated strength and power and I could feel the enormous authority it possessed. A Secret Service agent was stationed outside the room, which meant that it was a workday for the President. Just as I was leaving, President Bill Clinton himself walked into the Oval Office, whereupon Ms. Currie introduced me to him. My body felt a rush of adrenalin shoot through it as he gripped my hand. Suddenly I was that little boy from Arizona again, and I was meeting the 42nd President of the United States in the Oval Office of the White House! The President was laid back, calm, cool and collected, as he welcomed me to his White House staff. I now know how Clinton must have felt when he shook President Kennedy's hand in 1963 in the Rose Garden! We made some small talk, Betty handed the President his daily schedule, and then Betty and I left.

Betty is a kind, warm woman who sat me down in her office, ordered me some coffee and talked for what seemed an hour. She knew the importance of the Military Office to the President and she let me know that she was a phone call away if I ever needed her for anything. As I was leaving her office I got another surprise. Vice President Al Gore passed me and said hello as we passed. What an incredible day in my life. I know it sounds like I'm a gushing teenager who just met his music idol, but that's sort of what it felt like. I was thrilled! Who wouldn't be?

As the summer progressed I learned more of the inner workings of the White House. The staff was friendly and assisted me when I needed help. Across the hallway from my office was the Office of the Social Secretary, where Capricia Marshall and Laura Schwartz handled all the White House social events. When the President and First Lady Clinton hosted a formal event, our office supplied social aides for the event. These individuals were junior officers from all branches of service. The main idea was to make the event appear very formal with U.S. military officers present in their dress uniforms. These officers had to look sharp in uniform and were already screened with the Yankee White clearance. They worked in the D.C. area and were called when needed. A civilian in our office, Bobby Chunn, coordinated with Capricia Marshall to have the social aides available when needed. Bobby also coordinated with Debra Schiff to have two Marine sentries on duty at the West Wing entrance whenever the President was in the Oval Office.

One afternoon there was a Presidential press conference scheduled in the White House Press Room. Colonel Hawkins suggested I attend and sit in the back to observe our Communication Agency's handling of the affair. WHCA set up the public address system, filmed and archived the news conference, as they do for all Presidential events. The pressroom looked a lot larger on television, but still it was impressive. Before the President arrived, news correspondents were rushing around to ensure their network's feed was coming in live. At the one minute warning bright lights came on and the President's microphone went on as correspondents rushed to their seats like a game of musical chairs. There is a protocol for seating with the most senior correspondents up front. The front side door slid open as President Clinton walked in with some of his aides, the President took the podium and the aides sat just off stage to the side.

As I watched the news conference I saw notable correspondents, like the legendary Helen Thomas of the United Press International (UPI). After the President answered several tough questions and made some brief remarks, he left the podium and exited. The media personalities rushed outside to the North Lawn to give their live commentary on their respective networks, using the White House as a backdrop. The radio and print correspondents rushed to their workstations in the back of the room and were either on the phones or their computers frantically getting out any news that was made at the news conference. I again smiled as I observed all the commotion a brief 15-minute news conference can stir. As leader of the free world, every word is digested by the news media, to see if there is any news in what he just said.

In the fall of 1996, the President was rarely at the White House;

he was out campaigning for his second term. Alan Sullivan or Colonel Hawkins always traveled with the President to oversee the military support of the trip. Once we received the President's schedule, everyone went to work to see that airplanes and helicopters were ready and in place. A medical team, communications team and the President's military aides were ready to travel at a moment's notice. I would usually stay behind at the White House to handle things there. Back at the White House there was a sense of still, something in the air that said the President was not on the premises. Staff members seemed to be breathing a bit easier.

As you know, on November 5, 1996, President Clinton won re-election. He was the first Democrat to win re-election to the presidency since Franklin Roosevelt. The President's personal staff was thrilled with the win, but deep down several of us military members were secretly pulling for the World War II hero, Senator Bob Dole to win the election. But, the Republicans did maintain control of the Senate and House of Representatives. Once the election was over the President spent more time in Washington. This was a very good thing for our travel teams who were exhausted and welcomed the needed rest. We now went into planning mode for the Inauguration in January 1997.

Around that time, Luci and I were invited to a holiday reception at the White House scheduled for the evening of December 5th. We couldn't believe we were going to be attendees at a Christmas party hosted by the Clintons. I put on my best suit and Luci wore a beautiful white dress. When we arrived at the party, we were welcomed into the mansion by Capricia Marshall and escorted to the first floor of the residence, also called the State Floor because this is where formal receptions of state are held.

This floor includes the State Dining Room, East Room, Red Room, Blue Room, Green Room and the Cross Hall. There was a large spread of food, including a beautifully prepared Presidential turkey and prime rib being carved by a chef in full chef's attire, and a couple of cocktail bars at each end of the State Dining Room. With the Marine Corps band playing music in the background, Luci and I mingled in the Blue Room and made our way into the Red Room where we sat on an early nineteenth-century sofa.

Eventually we got up and looked out the window. From the other side of the fence people of all ages, ethnicities and types were trying their best to get a glimpse of what was going on inside the White House. It felt as if this were a dream! On the outside we were a nice, sophisticated, well-dressed couple attending a Presidential party, but on the inside it felt as if we should be on the other side of that fence looking in with the rest of the crowd. Luci and I whispered to each other that we didn't want the night to end as we feasted our eyes on all that went on around us and literally feasted on the wonderful food and drink set before us. We clicked our champagne glasses together and toasted each other and others in the room. This was a truly happy Christmas.

After about an hour, the Clintons came down from their residence and greeted everyone. They were like a regal couple, decked out in their best party attire. We all then moved into the East Room where a band was playing and we danced the night away. As the Presidential couple danced so too did Luci and I. We felt somewhat like royalty that night. Afterward, President and First Lady Clinton introduced themselves to Luci and shook her hand. I watched my wife's face. She was mesmerized by the whole affair. After dancing, we took pictures together. What an incredible evening for both of us. As the night came to an end, and when we got home, the twins wanted to know everything about the evening. We stayed up late with them telling them about our wonderful night. I looked out the window, half expecting our car to suddenly turn into a pumpkin and for Luci's beautiful dress to morph into Cinderella's rags. It was truly that magical of an evening.

At the Christmas party I met the Secretary of the Navy, the Honorable John J. Dalton. He invited me to be his and his wife's guest at the Army-Navy football game at Veterans Stadium in Philadelphia on December 8th. Of course I accepted and the next day his office at the Pentagon sent over two tickets. My brother-in-law Tom Farrell went with me to the game and it was great to see the two military powerhouses collide on the gridiron. President Clinton also attended the game. For the first half he sat with the Navy's fans, and during the second half he sat with the Army's fans. What a politician! Unfortunately, the Navy Midshipmen let an 18-point lead slip away, losing to the Army Cadets, 28-24.

I remember being a bit mesmerized by how beautifully the White House was decorated for Christmas. The theme that year was the Nutcracker Suite. A huge Colorado blue spruce tree from Coshocton, Ohio, adorned the Blue Room with all its lights and trimmings. The Blue Room is traditionally where the official White House Christmas tree stands. There were 36 other trees decorated throughout the White House. There was no way to forget the season! Volunteers would spend three days after Thanksgiving to decorate the entire White House to make it look so spectacular, and they did a bang-up job.

When 1997 came to D.C., the capital city was preparing for the 53rd Presidential Inauguration. The Inauguration Ceremony was held at the United States Capitol on Monday, January 20, 1997, at 11:30 a.m. Luci, Kristen, Kathy and I arrived early on a cold winter morning to watch the ceremony. To see the ceremony in person for the first time was an incredible experience. After it was over, I had tickets to watch the Inaugural Parade from the bleachers on the North Lawn of the White House. The whole day went flawlessly as President Clinton began his second four-year term, complete with all the pomp and circumstance his people could muster. That evening President and Mrs. Clinton celebrated at several inaugural balls throughout the D.C. area.

CHAPTER 35

The longer I worked at the White House the more routine I found my job to be. The entire White House Military Office staff performed at the highest levels. In March of 1997, the White House was preparing for the annual Easter Egg Roll on the South Lawn. The planning committee came to our office looking for a couple of young girls to dress up as Easter eggs and help entertain the children. I volunteered my daughters to dress up and help out with the festivities.

The Easter Egg Roll theme for the event was Learning is Delightful and Delicious. With a little prodding, I was able to get the twins to participate in this traditional White House event. They looked absolutely adorable in their Easter egg costumes as I took them onto the South Lawn with all the children who ran up to have their pictures taken with them. As the event progressed my office asked if I was willing to wear the Easter Bunny costume. The person that was supposed to wear the costume was unable to make the event, so I agreed and put on the full costume. The next morning in the Washington Post was a photograph of President and Mrs. Clinton with the children and the Easter Bunny. My claim to fame was that I made the paper, but no one knew who was under the costume. I guess the secret's out now!

On March 14, President Clinton was in Florida for a political event and spent the evening at the home of golf professional Greg Norman in Hobe Sound. Early in the morning the President suffered a torn ligament in his right knee when he missed a step in Greg Norman's backyard. In the dim light, the President thought he was on the walkway when, in fact, he had one more step to go. The President was rushed to a local hospital, where it was determined that he needed surgery.

I received a call in the early morning concerning the President's injury and we went into the planning phase to get the President back to D.C. There had not been an incident in recent history where a President could not walk up or down the stairs of Air Force One. We had no contingency device to help the President get on or off the aircraft. We were told specifically from the White House Chief of Staff that the President would not be carried off the aircraft. Such a sight would show weakness, so we came up with a truck that had a hydraulic power lift that was used for loading produce and fish into cargo aircraft. The only problem with the device was that it had a big fish market sign on the sides of the truck, but that was all we could find. Although it worked just fine to help the President get off Air Force One when he returned to Andrews Air Force Base, we were told to find a device without the fish market logo on the sides for his next trip. The President was due to fly to Helsinki the following weekend, so we quickly bought the loading truck and repainted the sides with the Presidential seal. The President was on crutches for eight weeks. He worked diligently with Connie and her White House medical team to get back to full strength. He was a trooper.

On May 1, 1997, a document came to our office from the U.S. Senate confirming the promotion of 90 Marine Corps Officers to the rank of Colonel. Navy Petty Officer Ron Wright, who worked in the WHMO office, handed me the document and said, "You may want to take a look at this." There in black and white was my name! I had been selected to the rank of Colonel. What a way to find out. I immediately called Luci and gave her the news. As a Colonel, I was now eligible to command a Marine Corps Air Group and get me back up in the air as a pilot, hopefully my next assignment.

The United States Military Academy in West Point, New York, was to have its graduation ceremony on Saturday, May 31, 1997, and the President was the guest speaker. This was a good time for me to watch the President on the road, and see how our travel team performed their duties. That morning, I boarded Air Force One for the first time at Andrews Air Force Base. Walking up the stairs and into the beautifully designed cabin was a thrill. Once inside I found my seat in the staff section, almost the size of a Lazy Boy recliner. I sat down, received a newspaper from the Air Force attendant, and just observed my surroundings. The staff section seated 8, with two rows of four seats facing each other, with a worktable in between. A large television screen was turned on with live cable news being broadcasted. Now, this is flying!

I had a lot of company on the flight, like Senator Jack Reed (D-RI), Representative John Shimkus (R-IL) and Representative Pete Sessions (R-TX) were seated in the guest section. White House staff members were seated in my section along with a couple Secret Service agents, and the White House Press Corps in the rear. We took off from Andrews AFB given all the priority we wanted as we took the runway with no delays. The mighty 747 went to full power as it made its way down the runway and into the air. Like a huge elephant with wings it soon made a left turn to head up the east coast toward New York. We landed an hour later at Stewart International Airport, New York. I then boarded a Marine Corps helicopter with other staff members and was taken to West Point for the graduation ceremony.

When I was in the air on Air Force One I went up into the cockpit and talked with the pilots. They gave me a brief of our route of flight. They were just ordinary guys in their Air Force blue uniforms doing their jobs as pilots. The Captain was Colonel Mark Donnelly who pointed out the various instruments and special features of the specially designed cockpit. While talking, I discovered he had grown up in Phoenix at the same time as I did. He grew up in central Phoenix and went to Central High School, only a few miles from Bourgade. Small world!! This would be the first of several flights for me on Air Force One. I would remember each with great detail and fondness.

Later that week, I received a framed certificate signed by the Presidential Aircraft Commander as a testament to my first flight on this prestigious aircraft. This was common practice for those flying for their first time on Air Force One. As a bonus, I received a set of six tumblers with the Air Force One Squadron Emblem engraved in the glass. Very cool!

CHAPTER 36

The Secretary General of the North Atlantic Treaty Organization (NATO) scheduled a NATO Summit on July 7-8, 1997, in Madrid, Spain. President Clinton and a large U.S. delegation were to attend the summit. I was the WHMO representative for this trip. We brought both of the Presidential 747s, leaving Andrews Air Force Base on July 5th. Our first stop was to Palma de Mallorca, the largest of the Spanish Balearic Islands in the Mediterranean, located just off the east coast of Spain. There the President enjoyed some down time in preparation for the NATO Summit. We then flew to Madrid for the two-day event, followed with stops in Warsaw, Bucharest and Copenhagen for diplomatic visits. On July 12th we flew back to the States. It was a seriously intense trip.

The planning and execution for such an expanded trip were also intense. Several USAF cargo planes (C-5s and C-141s) flew the necessary support equipment to the different locations we would hit. The President's limousines, helicopters, communication gear and Secret Service equipment all had to be pre-positioned and functioning at all locations. WHMO went into full planning mode when the trip was initially scheduled. My job was to see that everything went smoothly, which it did to my relief.

For me, to see our President with so many heads of state was humbling. Again, I had to pinch myself to see if this was real. In Poland, President Clinton met with the Polish President Aleksander Kwasniewski and former President Lech Walesa. In Bucharest, the President attended a reception hosted by President Emil Constantinescu at his Presidential palace, and in Copenhagen the President met with Queen Margrethe II and the Royal family at the Fredensborg palace. In 1972, Margrethe succeeded her father, Frederick IX, and became the first female monarch of Denmark since Margaret I, ruler of the Scandinavian countries in 1375 through 1412 during the Kalmar Union. Margrethe was a woman to be admired and respected. Aside from my love of flying, I adore history and world politics, and this trip indulged me in all of my passions.

We were back in Washington, D.C. for just five days and then headed off to Pittsburgh for the annual NAACP National Convention. Then it was on to Chicago for the National Association of Black Journalist (NABJ) Convention. On the flight, Jessie Jackson sat next to me and we had a nice conversation. While once again I had to pretend this was absolutely an everyday event for me as I was chatting with an American civil rights icon, and we were hitting it off just fine.

On a typical Presidential trip, we would manifest between 40 and 50 people on Air Force One. The President usually traveled with 10 to 15 staff members. Our office took roughly five people, and the Secret Service had between 10 and 15 agents. The press pool would compose of approximately 10 reporters. We comprised a large Presidential entourage. A Presidential motorcade usually included 20 to 25 brand new and very polished cars and vans. As we drove the streets to an event, local police officers shut down the roadway so the President could travel without interruption. Meanwhile, my personal entourage at home were growing and keeping busy.

As the summer of 1997 came to an end, Kristen and Kathy started high school at Robinson High School in Fairfax. They both decided to try out for the cheer squad and after several days of tryouts they both made the freshman team. They would cheer at all the football and basketball games. Many of their good friends were on the team with them. Remembering back to our move a couple of years earlier and how hard it had been for them at first, I was glad they were getting along so well with everyone now. They also participated in gymnastics and were big fans of the national girls' team from the 1998 Olympics. They both maintained a 4.0 academic average in the eighth grade and were looking to excel in high school. Michael was beginning his junior year at the University of Arizona, and was also doing very well. Life was good.

CHAPTER 37

In the fall of 1997, the President was off on several more trips. He loved to be in the limelight and in public to garner support for his political agenda. With Newt Gingrich as Speaker of the House of Representatives, many of the President's agenda items never made it out of committee. The President would usually have Congressmen to the Oval Office to gather support for his initiatives. I enjoyed watching them come and go from the White House. President Clinton had the knack with Congressional leaders to come to a compromise to get things done for the American people. The President signed landmark legislation by passing the Personal Responsibility and Work Opportunity Reconciliation Act, also known as Welfare Reform. The main goal of these reforms was to reduce the number of individuals or families dependent on government assistance and to assist the recipients in their efforts to become self-sufficient. The President's style of leadership was a model for me to emulate. I took mental notes I could use in future leadership roles.

One place President Clinton did not visit much was Camp David. I had to prod his personal aides to get him up there to take a break now and then. The main reason I wanted him there was for the Sailors and Marines who worked at Camp

David to feel appreciated. An occasional call to Betty was all it took to plant the seed in the President's head to take a break.

In late September 1997, on a Sunday morning, I was home watching Meet the Press. Attorney General Janet Reno was a guest. She said that she was concerned that the White House Communications Agency neglected to turn over videotapes of President Clinton's coffees with campaign contributors. That statement stirred a buzz around the White House.

White House Counsel Charles F.C. Ruff had requested all offices at the White House to turn over any items relating to Presidential coffee fundraisers in April 1997, because the Justice Department was conducting an investigation concerning political fundraising events held at the White House. I was the one who received the memo from the White House Counsel's office to have all agencies under the White House Military Office search for any documents or materials referring or relating to a number of subjects, including White House political coffees and Democratic National Committee fundraising meetings or events. Nowhere on the memo did I recall that the White House counsel asked for videotapes.

Within minutes after Meet the Press aired, my phone started ringing and my beeper went off. I knew this was trouble for our office and particularly for me. I was summoned to the White House to discuss this issue with Alan Sullivan. I located the memo. I was correct. It said nothing about videotapes. However, that didn't quite clear me, because just then a Sergeant who worked with me asked, "What about the attachment to the memo we put in the safe?"

Due to the sensitivity of some of the issues on the memo attachment I put it in our office safe. There were attachments to the memo I had forgotten about, so we quickly opened the safe to retrieve them. As I read it, there in black and white, it clearly stated "…request any and all videotapes relating to political coffees at the White House." I had never faxed the attachment to WHCA! That meant no one searched for any videotapes. It may have been an honest mistake, but it was a whopper.

In the hostile political world of Washington, D.C., there are always people ready to exploit an issue, no matter how trite, for political gain. I called WHCA and they later found 44 coffee videos that we handed over to White House counsel. The tapes were then turned over to Congressional and Justice Department investigators on October 4th. WHCA also found more than 100 other videotapes and audiotapes of DNC finance-related events. This soon made national news with congressional investigators accusing the Clinton Administration of a cover-up. And here I was in the middle of it all.

Our office soon received subpoenas to appear before congressional investigators for depositions, and the Republican leadership was asking for an independent counsel to investigate "Coffeegate." All I could think was, oh, my

God. Coffeegate?

I was assigned a military attorney to represent me at the deposition, but after Alan Sullivan and Steve Smith, Chief of Operations at WHCA, gave their depositions, I was never called in to give mine. Senator Fred Thompson's committee held hearings concerning this issue and the Deputy Director of WHCA, Colonel Campbell and Steve Smith testified that this was an honest mistake. Senator Lieberman of Connecticut, after hearing their testimony and after hearing all the acronyms used, such as WHCA and WHMO, said to Colonel Campbell, "You guys seem to be a bunch of wackos." He later apologized for that insensitive remark.

After the hearings and depositions, and with investigators finally viewing all the videotapes, the issue went away and things got back to normal at the office. That was an experience I never want to go through again, but I did learn a lot about Washington politics. To say the least I learned that politics, especially in D.C., is highly partisan and cutthroat. I was beginning to feel a bit jaded. The bloom was off the rose. Give me my F/A-18 back!

In mid-October, the President had the new Chairman of the Joint Chiefs of Staff, General Henry H. Shelton, USA, to the White House for a meeting. Our office usually coordinated meetings with Pentagon officials, acting as a liaison between the Pentagon and the White House. When the Chairman came by the White House I was able to meet him and talk with him while he waited. He seemed nervous, so I told him to relax. He smiled, took a breath and went into his meeting. I couldn't tell you what transpired there or why he was nervous, but I imagine meeting the President in the Oval Office would have anyone's nerves a bit frayed.

In November, the President traveled a lot to help fundraise for the Democratic Party. On one trip to Los Angeles, the pop singer Madonna held a private fundraiser at her home in Malibu. Those of us on the trip, to include the Secret Service, enjoyed listening to the singer entertain the President. As the President left her residence, everyone was trying to get pictures with Madonna and not with the President. It was amusing to watch. Clinton handled it in style. He didn't say a word.

The Marine Corps celebrated its 221st birthday on November 10, 1997 at the Sheraton Hotel in Alexandria, Virginia. The guest of honor was the Commandant of the Marine Corps, General Charles C. Krulak. I asked Betty Currie to bring her husband, and join Luci and me for the festivities. They accepted and we had a wonderful evening of dining and dancing.

The ballroom was adorned with Marine Corps battle pictures, pictures of famous Generals, and red, white and blue streamers. The meal was delicious, and after, it was time for a Marine Corps pageant with Marines dressed up in historical Marine Corps uniforms. They marched across the ballroom stage to the music of John Philip Sousa, the Bandmaster pre-eminent and composer of the early twentieth century. Then the Marine Corps Silent Drill Team came to the ballroom and put on their series of calculated drill movements and precise handling of their hand-polished M1 Garand rifles with fixed bayonets. Their routine concluded with a unique rifle inspection involving elaborate rifle spins and tosses. They received a standing ovation. Then the Marine Corps band played the National Anthem and Marine Corps Hymn as I stood proud with my hand over my heart, just like in first grade at St. Gregory's. The evening concluded with dancing, Luci even danced with the Secretary of Defense, The Honorable William Cohen. Betty and her husband had a fantastic time with us that evening, a welcome getaway from the grind of the Oval Office.

When I first arrived at the White House, a young White House Intern named Monica Lewinsky left for a position at the Pentagon. Rumors swirled around the White House that she had been "seeing" President Clinton in an improper relationship, but I dismissed this as just dirty pool. Then I heard from a Secret Service agent that former Vice President Mondale's daughter, Eleanor, had met with President Clinton at the White House in December 1997, while Monica Lewinsky was kept waiting at the White House gate for 40 minutes. During Lewinsky's wait, a Secret Service agent reportedly told her that Clinton was meeting with Eleanor Mondale, which prompted Miss Lewinsky to fly into a rage. The Washington Post reported that Lewinsky stormed away, and then proceeded to call and berate Betty Currie from a pay phone. After I heard about the incident, I knew there was something to the rumor, but I went about my business. I figure the situation had nothing to do with me or the security of our country, so why make a big deal out of it? Others in D.C. didn't share my point of view.

On December 18, Luci and I attended the annual holiday reception at the White House again. Like the previous year, we had a ball. The theme for the 1997 Christmas was Santa's Workshop, and the Blue Room was adorned with a beautiful Frasier Fur from Grassy Creek, North Carolina. Members of the National Needlework Association and Council of Fashion Designers of America joined with beautifully designed glass ornaments for the tree. The White House looked so beautiful all decked out for the holidays. The smell of fresh pine trees consumed the White House along with chocolate and peppermint from the many candy houses displayed throughout the State Floor.

Luci and I received a Christmas card from President and First Lady Clinton titled White House Nocturne, South Lawn 1997. The card had a picture of the White House in winter. Warm wishes were written inside and the card was signed, "Bill Clinton and Hillary Rodham Clinton." I keep this card in a scrapbook I put together after I left the White House and treat it as a treasure. It is but one treasure I've been fortunate in my life to attain. My Colonel eagles would be the next.

CHAPTER 38

On January 1, 1998, I received a message from Headquarters Marine Corps that I would receive my Colonel eagles. This was a big deal to me! Luci's mother came in from Pennsylvania, and on January 7th in the East Wing Reception Room of the White House, the Honorable Alan P. Sullivan recited my oath of office as I repeated it. Mr. Sullivan pinned an eagle on my left shoulder epaulet of my military jacket and Luci pinned on an eagle on my right shoulder epaulet. Kristen and Kathy each pinned on an eagle on each side of my shirt collar.

The Honorable Virginia M. Apuzzo, Assistant to the President for Management and Administration, along with several other guests attended the ceremony. We had a large chocolate cake with white frosting with the Marine Corps emblem and the words, "Congratulations, Colonel Raths," written on the cake with red frosting. After the ceremony I took Luci, her mother, and the twins to lunch at the White House Staff Dining Room. The President congratulated me later for my promotion, which added to how special I already felt about the event. For President Clinton to congratulate me in person meant the world to me. It meant he actually cared that I had received the honor and he was in tune with his staff.

An independent counsel, Kenneth Starr, was investigating President and First Lady Clinton at the time concerning allegations of misconduct at Mrs. Clinton's previous employment at the Rose Law Firm in Little Rock, Arkansas. It seemed like the hits just kept coming, but the Clinton's always took things in stride. They understood politics.

This investigation came to be known as "Whitewater." Starr was also looking into allegations of sexual harassment by then Governor Bill Clinton, during his 1992 Presidential campaign, with an Arkansas woman named Paula Jones. During a deposition conducted on January 17, 1998, before a judge concerning a federal civil rights action brought against President Clinton, he was asked if he ever had an extramarital sexual affair with Monica Lewinsky. He replied, "No."

Then he was asked if she had told someone that she had a sexual affair with him beginning in November of 1995. President Clinton was then asked, "Would that be a lie?"

The President replied, "It's certainly not the truth. It would not be the truth." This response garnered another question from Clinton's inquisitor.

"Have you ever had sexual relations with Monica Lewinsky?"

Clinton answered, "I have never had sexual relations with Monica Lewinsky. I've never had an affair with her." These false and misleading statements to a federal judge would lead to one of the largest sexual scandals in Presidential history. As most of us learned who were around at that time, providing a false and misleading statement before a federal judge is an impeachable offense. The President was on a slippery slope.

On January 21, 1998, The Washington Post reported that there are taped recording conversions of President Clinton and Monica Lewinsky, but the President dismissed this during an interview with Jim Lehr who was with PBS with a sentence recorded in history. He said, "There is no improper relationship."

Word around the White House at this time spoke to something different and we all figured that the President was in political trouble. We were instructed by White House Counsel not to comment to anyone concerning this matter unless subpoenaed. When I arrived home that evening Luci asked me what was going on with all this press about the President and an intern. I assured her it was nothing but rumor, although deep inside I knew this story had long legs.

Mrs. Clinton appeared on the NBC Today Show on January 27th and said this whole controversy has been fabricated by a "vast right-wing conspiracy." However, her denial of the issue continued to fuel the fire and the New York Times reported that Lewinsky met with President Clinton at the White House two weeks after she was subpoenaed to give information in the Paula Jones case, leading the press to believe the President had asked her to lie about their sexual encounters. I remember from the days of Watergate how President Nixon went into full denial and confined himself to the White House to stay out of the spotlight, but President Clinton went on with business as usual. He was a different type of animal entirely, cool as a cucumber always.

On January 28, I was working in my office with CNN muted on the television when I looked up and saw a Boeing 707 version of Air Force One stuck in the mud at an airport. At first I thought it was some file footage from years ago, but as I hit the un-mute button, the Presidential military aide who was on the trip with the President was on the phone for me. I knew the President was on a trip to Champaign, Illinois, that day and wondered what the call was about. The aide informed me that Air Force One was stuck in the mud at Willard Airport. The pilot had cut a corner too sharply while he was taxiing to the runway and went off into the mud.

I couldn't believe it. We had scheduled the smaller Boeing 707 for this trip for the sole purpose that the Boeing 747 was too large for that airport. We had another airplane in the air immediately to pick up the stranded President and passengers. President Clinton took it all in stride commenting, "What are you going to do?" Within a couple of hours he was on his way to La Crosse, Wisconsin, for a political rally. I admired how Clinton took things in stride. I sometimes wondered if anything could rattle that man. I got my answer soon enough.

My buddy John Daly was visiting me at the White House not long after the airplane incident. As I showed him around we walked by the Oval Office and heard the President talking with a senator. Their voices carried out into the hallway. The President was saying, "...this was not an impeachable offense." My friend and I looked at each other and knew that the President was very concerned about the Lewinsky issue. With the scandal growing, ABC news brought the veteran newsman Sam Donaldson back as a White House correspondent to cover the story.

On February 3rd, I was assigned to a Presidential trip to the Los Alamos National Laboratory in New Mexico where the President was to view a new supercomputer. As the President passed the press pool in Los Alamos, Sam Donaldson yelled out, "MR. PRESIDENT, TELL US ABOUT MONICA!"

The President ignored Donaldson and kept walking. Visibly upset, White House staff member Doug Sosnik looked at Presidential Advisor Bruce Lindsey. Sosnik said under his breath, "Can you believe that jerk is back with the press pool." I smiled a little as I heard this exchange. What did they expect?

CHAPTER 39

During our trip at Los Alamos, a U.S. Marine Corps EA-6B aircraft flying out of Aviano Air Base, Italy, was on a low-level training mission in northeast Italy and severed a gondola cable at a ski resort, sending 20 passengers to their deaths. Nine women, ten men and one child were killed when the gondola plunged about 300 feet onto the mountainside. The President asked me how such a tragedy could occur. I told him at a high speed and low level it is very hard to see cables that size, but it should have been indicated on a map. Our White House Communications Office representative on the trip immediately, as instructed, got the Prime Minister of Italy, Romano Prodi, on the phone for President Clinton to express his condolences and pledge full U.S. cooperation in the accident investigation. It was clear to me that the President truly was deeply moved by the incident. I overheard him tell Prodi, "We will do everything we can to find out what happened and prevent an accident like this from happening again. On behalf of the American people I offer my heartfelt sympathy to the families and friends of those killed and injured in this accident." And he did just that.

Not too long after this, my son graduated from the University of Arizona. That was in May of 1998. I'm proud to report that he also received his officer's commission as a Second Lieutenant in the Marine Corps. Luci and I had the honor of pinning on his Second Lieutenant gold bars at the commissioning ceremony at the university. My parents joined us for the ceremony to witness a third generation of Raths men to become a military officer. Mike went on to Quantico for six months of basic officer training and then off to Pensacola for flight training. During his six months in Quantico he would come by our home often. We really had a chance to bond, swapping stories of training and the people at the helm.

In D.C, the Lewinsky scandal continued to grow and the President continued to deny a sexual involvement with her. Rumors were going around the White House that the President was going to resign and that Vice President Gore was preparing his team to take over the presidency. I didn't believe what I was hearing. President Clinton was a fighter and would not go down so easily. As accusations grew, the President went about his business and continued to travel around the country for different events. The Republican House of Representatives, led by Speaker Newt Gingrich (R-GA), pounced on this scandal though it was later determined that he himself was having an extramarital affair with one of his staff members at the same time. Ah, politicians. They have their own set of rules, don't they? Nevertheless, Gingrich and other Republican leaders, such as Representative Henry J. Hyde (R-IL), were pushing for Articles of Impeachment against the President.

On July 28, 1998, Lewinsky received an immunity deal with Ken Starr, and she made public that she had a semen stain on a blue dress she wore when she was with the President during a sexual encounter. The smoking gun may just have been revealed.

The FBI ordered a DNA sample of the President by means of a blood test. On August 3rd, at 10:10 p.m. in the Map Room of the White House, Dr. Connie Mariano drew blood from the President's right arm in the presence of three witnesses. On August 17th, the FBI lab determined with an 8 trillion-to-1 conclusion that the DNA was that indeed of President Clinton. That morning, the White House Chief of Staff Erskine Bowles sent a memo to all White House offices that the President would address the nation, and the news was not good. He urged all staff members to support the President under such difficult circumstances. That evening the President went live on national television and stated, "As you know, in a deposition in January, I was asked questions about my relationship with Monica Lewinsky. While my answers were legally accurate, I did not volunteer information. Indeed, I did have a relationship with Ms. Lewinsky that was not appropriate. In fact, it was wrong. It constituted a critical lapse in judgment and a personal failure on my part for which I am solely and completely responsible. But I told the grand jury today and I say to you now that at no time did I ask anyone to lie, to hide or destroy evidence or to take any other unlawful action. I know that my public comments and my silence about this matter gave a false impression. I misled people, including even my wife."

The Clintons had planned to leave on their summer vacation the next day to Martha's Vineyard. Everyone was busy speculating about whether they would go on vacation as a family. Our office was told to have the Presidential helicopter ready that afternoon on the South Lawn for departure to Andrews AFB.

When the President usually leaves on a trip from the South Lawn there are a handful of reporters to cover the event. That afternoon the entire White House Press Corps was out to see how this departure would unfold. Finally, after a few minutes, the President strode from the Diplomatic Reception Room onto the South Lawn clutching the hand of his daughter, Chelsea, who in turn held hands with her mother. Their brown Labrador, Buddy, was also in tow. At that moment I felt empathy for the President, but I also knew he brought this on himself. Mrs. Clinton was stoic. She would be criticized in the papers, but she held fast to her convictions. She also remained married to Bill.

With the First Family away on vacation things would be quiet at the White House. At least that's how it usually went when they were away. However, on the morning of August 20th, I received a call from the President's military aide saying that the President would be coming back to the White House. My first thought was that Hillary had kicked him out of Martha's

Vineyard, but later that morning President Clinton called a press conference there to announce a military strike against installations associated with suspected terrorist Osama bin Laden.

The President claimed that he had received compelling information that Bin Laden was planning terrorist attacks against U.S. citizens and others around the world. He stated that "America will protect its citizens and will continue to lead the world's fight for peace, freedom and security. I am returning to Washington to be briefed by my National Security team on the latest information."

Clinton was correct about the information but was off on the timing. As we all know, Bin Laden was behind the attack three years later on September 11, 2001. Our world would never be the same. Today, as I write this, our country is still working its way back from the damage that attack perpetrated on the American mindset. While Clinton was on watch against terrorist attack, he was on guard against personal and political attack on U.S. soil.

October 8, 1998, by a vote of 258 to 176 (with 31 Democrats voting yes) the House of Representatives approved an open-ended impeachment inquiry of the President. The White House counsel team of William Ruff and Cheryl Mills represented the President who was charged with obstruction of justice and then separately charged with committing perjury. An air of doom and gloom wafted through the halls of the White House, but that didn't stop President Clinton from going about his daily business. He had a lot to attend aside from fighting off allegations. For example, on October 29th, Senator John Glenn was scheduled to take off from Cape Canaveral on the shuttle Discovery along with six other astronauts. I accompanied the President and felt proud to stand by his side as we watched the shuttle thunder off the launch pad, shaking the ground beneath our feet. We watched it until we could see no more trace of the shuttle as it made its way into space that clear Florida afternoon.

President Clinton wasn't just about vacations and having a presence at newsworthy events. He traveled a lot for many reasons. I don't know if the general public knows just how many near disasters President Clinton helped our country to avoid. He was one heck of a diplomat. I don't think I realized that fact until I saw him in action and heard about his diplomatic skills from staff around the White House. For example, Clinton was a major player in the peace talks in the Middle East in early December of 1998. That's when he scheduled a trip to the Middle East to lead peace talks with Israeli Prime Minister Benjamin Netanyahu and the Palestine Liberation Organization Chairman Yasser Arafat. I went along.

On December 12th, Air Force One took off from Andrews Air Force Base. A day after we arrived, President Clinton first met with Benjamin Netanyahu at his office in Jerusalem, and later that day visited the gravesite of Prime Minister Yitzhak Rubin at Mount Herzl. That evening Clinton went to Beit Hanassi to meet the Israeli President Ezar Weizman and attend a candle-lighting ceremony for the first day of Chanakah, and then later met for dinner with Benjamin Netanyahu. Clinton's stamina amazed me. I was tired and I wasn't the diplomat!

The following day the President boarded Marine One in Jerusalem and flew to Gaza International Airport where he was greeted by Chairman Arafat and his wife Souha. He would then have a bilateral meeting with Arafat to discuss terms of peace in the Middle East. That afternoon Arafat hosted a luncheon at Zahrat Al Madean, commonly known as the Flower of the City. After the luncheon, the President finally had a chance to rest in the guest palace. His next event would be at the Shawa Center where he would address the Palestinian National Council and other organizations. We were to arrive at 3:45 in the afternoon, but while we were at the guest palace, President Clinton took a nap. I was in the staff room with the other Presidential staffers when I noticed the time. Clinton was late! It was already 4:00. "Isn't any one going to wake up the President for his next activity?" I asked, looking around the room. It wasn't my place to wake the man, but apparently no one else wanted to take on the duty either. Finally, his personal aide, Kirk Hamlin, went and woke him. Good thing, because we were really running behind. I guess even Presidents have to sleep sometimes.

After the address it was off to Matak Headquarters in Israel where the President had a trilateral meeting with Prime Minister Netanyahu and Chairman Arafat. The meeting, which was scheduled for an hour and a half, went well into the night as the three leaders discussed peace. I received phone calls from the Marine One pilot asking when the meeting would wrap up for the night. He was anxious because they were well over their crew day to fly. They would have to wait like the rest of us. I was told by a Presidential staffer the meeting could go all night, and if the Marine pilots were too tired to fly the President back to Jerusalem, then I should find an Israeli helicopter and crew to get him back. I was dumbstruck by the suggestion.

"Are you telling me, you want the President of the United States to fly in an Israeli helicopter with an Israeli aircrew?" I said, and then quickly answered myself. "Absolutely not! Only United States Military helicopters with Marine Corps pilots will fly our President." I was surprised by the force of my own words. I made an executive decision and I was sticking by it. I called the Marine One pilot and told him to have his crew rest in their helicopter until the meeting concluded. Everyone on the President's staff was exhausted, and I understood why the staffer made such a reckless request. The meeting did finally end early in the morning and we were able to get the President safely back to Jerusalem on Marine One.

The next day would be a busy one, too. President and First Lady Clinton were scheduled to fly to Bethlehem and visit the Church of the Nativity that morning. They were airlifted to Bethlehem on Marine One, but since there was limited space on the helicopter I took a taxi to meet them there. I was unaware that there would be a number of armed Palestinian checkpoints along the way. My cab was stopped several times and searched by some very shady gunmen with their faces covered with Palestinian headscarves. They interrogated me asking who I was and why I was on this road. I showed them my Presidential credentials, but that didn't seem to mean anything to these men. I asked the cab driver if this was normal and he replied, "I don't think these guys like Clinton or any American for that matter."

"Now you tell me," I responded. At this moment, I feared for my life as we progressed slowly to Bethlehem. Would this become an international incident? Was I in real danger? I sure felt I was as I looked down the barrel of a Russian made AK-47 and into the piercing eyes of these militiamen.

After what seemed like an eternity I arrived in Bethlehem and found the opening to the Church of the Nativity, where a Secret Service agent I knew let me in. I was never so relieved to see that agent. Once in the church, I joined the Presidential tour of the birth site of Jesus. For a Catholic boy like me, this was a treat.

Chairman Arafat and his wife, along with Greek Orthodox, Armenian and Franciscan Patriarchs of the church, led the tour. We came to the place allegedly where the manger was when Christ was born and I felt a calm go through my body, a spiritual feeling that I cannot adequately describe. I kneeled down and said a few prayers, and with only one life of the infamous nine lives left, I asked the Lord to keep me safe when I went back to flying.

As we left the church, in a barren dirt courtyard surrounded by ancient buildings and people hanging out the windows to get a glimpse of the Presidential entourage, President Clinton lit a large decorated Christmas tree while a children's choir sang, Oh, Little Town of Bethlehem. Here I was in the old country, where Christianity began, and I took it all in. The large tree that adorned St. Gregory's at Christmas when I was a kid did not hold a candle to this magnificent tree as it sparkled.

We left Bethlehem on a Marine Corps helicopter and flew to a landing zone near the Dead Sea to climb the Masada, a fortress that is an ancient site of palaces and fortifications on top of an isolated rock plateau on the eastern edge of the Judean Desert. The Masada looks over the Dead Sea. This Masada is best known for the violence that occurred there in the first century when the first Jewish-Roman war was waged.

Most of the Presidential staff hiked up the path on the eastern side of the mountain, but the Clintons took a cable car to the top. As a history buff, to experience this ancient site and that period in history was amazing for me. Things I had read in books came alive in front of my eyes. I didn't have a chance to spend too much time pondering history in this magnificent place, because pretty quickly we were zipping off to Ben-Gurion International Airport, where we took off on Air Force One for the 12-hour flight back to D.C. It was pretty clear by the expression on the President's face from time to time during that flight that he wasn't looking forward to getting back to the Capital City. After all, that's where his critics were waiting to once again pounce. They weren't done berating him about the Lewinsky fling.

On the flight home I noticed the President was on the secure radios longer than usual. My thought was that he should be getting some rest. On the day after we landed I found out why he was on the radios. On December 16, the entire nation would know. That's the day the American public would hear an introduction to the words "Saddam Hussein" and "weapons of mass destruction," together. I will never forget the President's speech that night. I recall it word for word, and I knew our country was in for some bad road ahead.

"Good evening," the President said, beginning his address. "Earlier today I ordered America's Armed Forces to strike military and security targets in Iraq. They are joined by British forces. Their mission is to attack Iraq's nuclear, chemical and biological programs and its military capacity to threaten its neighbors. Their purpose is to protect the national interest of the United States and, indeed, the interest of people throughout the Middle East and around the world. Saddam

Hussein must not be allowed to threaten his neighbors or the world with nuclear arms, poison gas, or biological weapons. I want to explain why I have decided, with the unanimous recommendation of my national security team, to use force in Iraq, why we have acted now, and what we aim to accomplish. The international community had little doubt then, and I have no doubt today, that left unchecked, Saddam Hussein will use these terrible weapons of mass destruction."

For a President whom was under threat of being impeached, he sure didn't show any signs that he was concerned about such matters. Obviously, there were bigger fish to fry. And just two days later, the House of Representatives approved two articles of impeachment against the President. Thus, President Clinton became only the second President in American history to be impeached while in office. The next stage would be a trial in the U.S. Senate, overseen by the Chief Justice of the Supreme Court, William Rehnquist. The trial began on January 7, 1999. It went on for about four weeks. On February 12, 1999, President Clinton was found not guilty on both counts. You could almost hear a collective sigh of relief from everyone at the White House. This nightmare was finally over.

During the days of the impeachment trial, there was a tornado that caused extensive damage in Little Rock, Arkansas. The tornado actually caused damage to the governor's mansion that President Clinton once occupied when he was governor of that state. The event must have touched Clinton deeply, because not long after he flew to Little Rock to survey the damage. As usual, I accompanied him. The damage caused by the storm was incredible to behold. As we toured the damaged areas, trees were uprooted, homes gone from their foundations, and cars tossed around like tinker toys littered the area. The President stopped and talked and consoled hurting people, reassuring them that the federal government would do all it could to help the survivors. He expressed his condolences to those families that lost loved ones or property. While the President spoke to the crowd I heard in my earpiece from a Secret Service agent that Paula Jones was in the audience. Here she was, the lady who went public about an alleged sexual harassment charge against the President, and she was just a few yards away from him. What now, I thought?

In a heartbeat all eyes were on Ms. Jones. The Secret Service agents were concerned that she would start some sort of upheaval, but she remained quiet and walked away with the crowd after the President had finished speaking. She later said that she was just a concerned citizen interested in what the President would say about the tornado damage. I couldn't help but think that she was much like a tornado in Clinton's life.

CHAPTER 40

A personal friend of the President, Carolyn Huber, Special Assistant to the President in charge of personal correspondence, worked down the hall from my East Wing office. She was leaving the White House to return to Little Rock and to her private life. The President held a small farewell party for her in the Yellow Oval Room upstairs in the White House residence. Our office was invited, and I was excited, because I always wanted to see the second floor of the mansion. Odd as it may sound, I hadn't ever seen it, since this was the personal space for the First Family and seldom were visitors invited up there.

From the Oval Yellow Room I walked out on the Truman Balcony that overlooked the South Lawn. The view of Washington, D.C. was spectacular from that vantage point. I could see several monuments, like the Washington Monument and the Jefferson Memorial. In fact, they were in full view. After the farewell party, the President's valet gave us a personal tour of the second floor, which included the Lincoln Bedroom, the Queen's Bedroom and the Treaty Room. Until that moment, those rooms were just words or pictures in books to me. I had read about them, but to be standing in these rooms made me feel special.

The Lincoln Bedroom is located in the southeast corner of the second floor, part of a guest suite that includes the Lincoln Sitting Room. The rooms are named for Abraham Lincoln, and the room was used by President Lincoln as an office. The central feature of the room is the Lincoln bed, a nearly 8-foot by 6-foot rosewood bed with an enormous headboard, which is believed to have been purchased by Mary Todd Lincoln during her extensive redecorating efforts. The bed was probably never used by President Lincoln, although several later Presidents have used it. An ornamental crown-shaped canopy hood was recently reconstructed to replace the lost original. As we were leaving the room I quickly sat on the bed to claim to my friends that I sat on the Lincoln bed in the White House.

The Queen's Bedroom, located across the center hall from the Lincoln Bedroom is a guest suite that includes the Queen's Sitting Room. It is named for the many royal guests it has hosted, including queens of the Netherlands, Greece, Norway, Nepal and the United Kingdom. The bed thought to have belonged to Andrew Jackson is used here. It was donated in 1902 and first used in what is today the Lincoln Bedroom. Again I was the last to leave as I wasn't in a hurry. I was busy just taking it all in.

We then walked upstairs to the third floor where we were shown the President's music room. It was filled with his private collection of saxophones that he actually played and other musical instruments. The walls were covered with several autographed photographs and framed record albums of notable musicians, including Kenny G and Sheryl Crow. Several pictures were of the President with the respective musicians playing their music instruments together. In fact, on President Clinton's 52nd birthday, Sheryl Crow came to the White House and sang to the President her famous song, All I Wanna Do. I smiled inside as I heard the lyrics:

> All I want to do is have a little fun before I die
> Says the man next to me out of nowhere
> It's apropos of nothing he says his name is William
> But I'm sure he's Bill or Billy or Mac or buddy
> And he's plain ugly to me, and I wonder if he's ever
> Had a day of fun in his whole life…

From my observations, Bill was having plenty of fun being President of the United States. One room on the third floor that I didn't know existed is the Solarium, or Sun Room which provides a 270 degree view of Washington, D.C., President Clinton used this room as a game room, with board games scattered throughout the room.

I would have a lot of stories to share with my folks next time I saw them, which wasn't far into the distant future. I would be seeing them at my dad's World War II Air Group reunion in Norfolk, Virginia, in September. Luci and I joined them at the banquet on the final day of the reunion and we enjoyed talking with my dad's war buddies. I learned a lot about my dad and the dangerous missions he flew while he was in Europe. Since I am a fighter pilot, I could appreciate the stories in a new light.

My dad's aircrew men were there and told me how great a pilot my dad was during the war. It was sobering to hear all their stories. After the reunion my parents stayed at our house for a few days and I was able to take them on a tour of the White House and then to lunch. They got an extra treat, too. The President walked up to them along the colonnade near the West Wing and said hello. You should have seen my parents' faces. Their expressions were priceless, like I had given them the coolest gift ever. I admit it was a lucky break to have Clinton walk past when he did, but to see how much it tickled my mother was great. At the time, she was just beginning to show signs of dementia. She recognized the President, but she had trouble remembering who I was. She kept calling me Bob (my brother) and asking me questions that made little sense. Later, Alzheimer's would take the rest of her memories and she would become helpless. This is how it was until the end of her life. I would lose my mother on September 11, 2007. She was 88 years old. If she had taught me anything it was to be a good citizen and that change was the only constant. It certainly seemed that way around the White House.

Alan Sullivan left his position as Director of the White House Military Office in December 1998 and Colonel Simmons of

WHCA took the position as the new Director, once he retired from active duty. When he took his oath of office, as an African American, it was an extremely proud moment for him. He asked me to stay on as his Chief of Staff, but I had just received notice from Headquarters Marine Corps that I had been selected to command of a Marine Aircraft Group at MCAS, Miramar in San Diego, California. I was to take command of Marine Aircraft Group 46 (MAG-46) on the 45th anniversary of D-Day, June 6, 1999. I would have to depart the White House in March to prepare for command. MAG-46 was a composite air group that had several squadrons of aircraft, including helicopters. I would need the three months from March to June to train in the various aircraft I would be flying. Fortunately for me, HMX-1 in Quantico flew both the CH-46 and CH-53 helicopters, so I spent a couple of weeks in Quantico training in those helicopters. It felt good to get back in control of an aircraft.

On my final trip on Air Force One, the White House staff members on the trip surprised me with a farewell cake and ice cream in the President's conference room on the plane. Admittedly, that was pretty cool. President Clinton had the Secretary of Transportation, Rodney E. Slater, as a guest on the flight. Not everyone can say they had cake and ice cream with the likes of these men. I was honored.

On my last day of work at the White House I had one more honor. I was to meet with the President in the Oval Office with my family. He had invited us to take some pictures with him and wanted to say his goodbyes. My daughters gave him a green frog Beanie Baby as a gift. You may not know this, but our President Clinton collected frog memorabilia. My girls thought it would be fun to give him one for his collection. He sure seemed to appreciate the gesture. Most of the time, the President came across as a pretty average guy. He was never pompous. I truly enjoyed working on his staff and I would miss my duties at the White House.

As we were about to leave the Oval Office, Kathy asked the President, "How's your dog, Buddy?"

The President said, "Let me find him for you." In that moment, Clinton was just a normal guy, a pet owner… someone who obviously adored his dog. The President walked out the side door of the Oval Office onto the patio near the Rose Garden yelling, "GLENN, GLENN, GET BUDDY OVER HERE." Glenn was the dog's trainer.

Seconds later, the big brown lab came running up to us all. My girls were delighted. We joined the President on the patio as they covered the dog with affection and the President talked about how he always loved dogs and how he had several dogs when he was a young boy. The entire event took about ten minutes, but it remains one of the most memorable for my family and me. I guess you might say it was heartwarming.

After our visit with the President we returned to the Military

Office for my farewell party. The Honorable Joseph Simmons pinned on the Defense Superior Service Medal for my service at the White House. Secretary of Defense, William S. Perry, had signed the citation and sent along a note thanking me for my service to our country. I sometimes look at that citation and wonder where time went. It seems like yesterday that I was working at the White House. Ah, but time has a way of marching on.

AFTERWARD

LIFE AFTER THE WHITE HOUSE

My life thus far has been amazing. I wrote this book to share my experiences and show how I achieved the American dream so that I can help others see that they can achieve the same; they too can strive for excellence in their lives. If this little boy who grew up in the southwest city of Phoenix could grow up to rise to the top of his profession and contribute significantly to American society as a patriot and then to work at the White House, so can young men and women of today.

I trained to become a fighter pilot, and I loved that life. I became a member of the White House staff under President Clinton, and I loved that life, too. But what happened between that life and now? I'm glad you asked. I end this book with a two-chapter summary.

CHAPTER 41

My days at the White House now over, it was once again time for me to get back to my profession, flying airplanes. My family was looking forward to returning to southern California, even though the twins had grown close to a new circle of friends in Fairfax. Our plan was for me to head to San Diego to refresh in the F/A-18 Hornet, and Luci and the twins would stay in Fairfax until school was over in late May.

When I arrived at MCAS Miramar it felt good to climb back into the cockpit of a jet fighter. At age 47, I had to stay physically and mentally sharp when I flew such a high-performance jet. I would have to train a little harder than when I was a young pilot. I trained for two months and completed everything necessary in time for the Change of Command Ceremony on June 6, 1999.

My dad, mom, brothers Bob and Dan, and my sister Jean came to the ceremony to celebrate the event with me. My little family was there, too. My dad wore his World War II Army Air Corps uniform and looked rather dapper. I could tell he was proud to wear the uniform and proud of me. I wish every man could experience the approval of his father. It's something that makes an impression in life. My son, Mike, was there in his uniform, and all three generations of Raths military officers were on display in full military attire.

At the end of the ceremony as the Marines from the squadrons passed in review, my dad joined me and the outgoing commanding officer, Colonel Gary Gisolo, to observe the troops march past us. My former White House boss, Alan Sullivan, my math teacher from high school, Father Rodenspiel, Jim O'Connor's brothers Dan and Tim, and my cousin Marie and her family were also at the ceremony to celebrate that important day with me.

MAG-46 comprised of more than 1,000 Marines and 70 aircraft spread across four locations in the Pacific southwest. The group's headquarters were at MCAS Miramar in San Diego, along with VMFA-134, an F/A-18 Hornet squadron, MALS-46, a Marine Aviation Logistics squadron, MASS-6, a Marine Air Support squadron, MWSS-473, a Marine Wing Support squadron, and MWCG-48, a Marine Wing Control Group detachment. At MCAS Yuma, Arizona, was VMFT-401, an F-5E Tiger II Aggressor squadron. At MCAS Camp Pendleton, California, was based HMLA-775, an AH-1W Super Cobra and UH-1N Huey helicopter squadron, and at Edwards AFB, northeast of Los Angeles, was HMH-769, a CH-53E Super Stallion helicopter squadron and HMM-764 a CH-46E Sea Knight helicopter squadron. This was the largest composite air group in the Marine Corps at the time. I remember Colonel Rietsch telling me during Desert Storm when he commanded MAG-11 that it was good to be king, and so it was for me now, too. I knew fully what he meant as I worked this assignment. It would last for two years and I would enjoy every minute of it.

I moved my family back into our home in Orange County so the twins could be near their old friends. They enrolled for their junior year of high school at Capistrano Valley High School, in Mission Viejo. They tried out for cheerleading, but the competition was too great for them to make the squad. Luci went to work at California State University, Fullerton, as a lecturer for the Education Department. I commuted to San Diego and arrived each day, bright and early, to oversee the air group's operations. Some would ask me if I ever grew tired of the long commute. My answer is no, because I loved what I did so much that the drive was unimportant. It was just something I had to do at the time. The drive gave me time to think about what I had to do when I arrived on base.

The best way to see what was happening at a squadron was to visit the units and fly a training mission with them. During the briefing, training flight, and debriefing I would learn how the squadron functioned first hand, and I could easily determine morale, professionalism or any problems that existed, plus I remained current in the squadron's specific aircraft. On Mondays I would stay at the headquarters for administrative issues, but on Tuesdays I would jump into an F/A-18 and fly to MCAS Yuma for a training mission in the F-5 Tiger II. The next day I would fly to Edwards AFB to visit my helicopter units and fly a couple training missions with them. On Thursday I would take my Hornet into MCAS Camp Pendleton and fly some training missions in the Cobra and Huey helicopters. By Friday I was home at Miramar to wrap up the week at the headquarters. My executive officer, Lt. Col. Ken Jorgensen, held down the fort while I was on the road. Friday night Luci would meet me at the Officer's Club to unwind over a cold drink, but on weekends I was home with my girls in Mission Viejo. It was a hectic schedule, but I loved it. I was in the catbird seat, living a pilot's dream.

Every Colonel that is in a command position has an adjutant office that prepares the commander's weekly schedule. My adjutant, Captain Adzekai Kuma, was the best when it came to taking care of the minute details of my schedule. She was assisted by Gunnery Sergeant Cynthia Manderfield and Staff Sergeant Lisa Leighton, both top-notch professionals. I gave these three the title, "The Colonel's Angels," because they watched over me and kept me on a tight schedule and out of trouble.

To keep the morale high at the headquarters I would, on occasion, take the staff to Hawaii, Las Vegas and/or New Orleans on a KC-130 for some needed time away. The KC-130 pilots at Miramar were always conducting training flights, and if I saw an interesting destination that they planned to visit, I loaded my staff on the aircraft and off we'd go. A benefit of being in the military is the privilege to fly space available on military aircraft.

My time at MAG-46 moved quickly. As the year 2000 approached Y2K, or the Millennium Bug, was on everyone's minds. They feared problems for both digital and non-digital computers and data storage situations that resulted from the practice of abbreviating a four-digit year to two digits. We prepared all our computers and data cards on all the aircraft for this approaching problem, too. Fortunately, the year 2000 arrived with only minor, easily fixable problems.

As the 21st Century became a reality, I found myself interested in the 2000 Presidential race between Texas Governor George W. Bush and Vice President Al Gore. All predictions and polling indicated a very tight race between these two political titans. Luci and I sat up late to watch the results, and when NBC political commentator Tom Brokaw reported that the counting of votes, especially in Florida, was too close to call, I knew our country was in for a difficult period. We wondered about the political machine at the heart of the election when we heard about the controversy concerning Florida's 25 electoral votes and who they would go to.

With the presidency hanging on a few hundred votes in Florida, there were lawsuits and requests for recounts. The punch card ballots posed a major problem as many ballots were called into question because voters failed to punch a hole all the way through the ballot. The word "chad" entered the American vocabulary. In an extraordinary late-night decision, the U.S. Supreme Court halted a recount ordered by the Florida Supreme Court. A narrow majority of the Justices said that the recount ordered by the Florida Supreme Court violated the principle that all votes must be treated equally. It also ruled that there was not enough time to conduct a new count that would meet constitutional muster. Five weeks after Election Day 2000, the Republican candidate, Texas Governor George W. Bush was declared the 43rd President of the United States, the first President since 1888 to win the presidency without winning the popular vote. George Bush did win 30 of the 50 states, however.

On January 20, 2001, George W. Bush, son of the 41st President of the United States, George H.W. Bush, was sworn into office in Washington, D.C. I had to smile as I thought of all the new staff members the new President would bring with him from Texas to the White House, and all the Arkansas staffers were gone and back to their prior jobs and professions.

Hillary Clinton ran for Senator of New York in 2000 and won, marking the first time an American First Lady had run for public office. Mrs. Clinton was also the first female senator to represent the state of New York. The Clintons made their residence in Chappaqua, New York. President Clinton moved into offices to Harlem, New York, where he set up shop for his post-presidency life. From what I knew of him, he would have a difficult time transitioning to everyday life. He would miss the limelight and all the prestige that went with the presidency.

At this time I was enjoying my tour with MAG-46. During the Christmas season every year my CH-46E squadron from Edwards AFB, would help out with the Toys for Tots program by flying toys down to the Indians in the Havasupai Canyon in Arizona. The Flagstaff chapter of the Marine Corps League would gather toys for the American Indian children and we assisted them by flying the toys down to the bottom of the canyon. We received permission from Headquarters Marine Corps to take several of the civilians from the Marine Corps League down with us on the helicopter to help distribute the toys; one was dressed up as Santa Claus. The CH-46E troop carrier could accommodate about 25 people and we loaded them up with boxes of wrapped toys. I had my dad and brother Bob drive up from Phoenix and they came along with us down the canyon with me at the controls of the helicopter. What a fantastic feeling to be flying my dad in the back of the helicopter. We landed and shut down the engines and spent about two hours passing out toys and singing Christmas songs to the children. It is times like this that made me so proud of my profession.

As my time was winding down at MAG-46, a new commanding officer had been selected to take command in August 2001, so I had a few more months to enjoy the assignment as the "king." Kristen and Kathy graduated from high school in May, and they were both selected as their class valedictorian with a GPA of 4.0 each. It was a proud day for me to see my daughters receive their diplomas. Their plan was to attend Saddleback Valley Community College in Mission Viejo for two years and then to San Diego State University. They both wanted to be elementary school teachers, so they selected liberal arts as their major. Mike was now in flight school in Pensacola, Florida doing very well. He decided to go the route of a Naval Flight Officer, the aviator that works the systems in the rear seat of the two-seat F/A-18D. He worked hard to get his own set of gold wings.

When my tour ended and I passed command to Colonel William R. Liston it was a beautiful, sunny afternoon on the flight deck at MCAS Miramar. It was difficult to leave all the Marines I grew so close to over the past two years. As a career military officer, I knew this was the process of a career path. I was assigned to the MCAS Miramar Commanding General's staff as his Chief of Staff for Administration. The base was commanded by Major General William Bowdon, an F/A-18 pilot himself. Just over a month after I took this new position, the events of September 11, 2001 splashed across the headlines. The Miramar base went immediately into full lock down. No one was allowed to enter or leave the base. After a couple of hours to digest the news, General Bowden reopened the gates to get necessary personnel on base, but only after a thorough inspection of their vehicles.

The Emergency Command Center on base was immediately activated and staffed with base personnel. F/A-18s were loaded with air-to-air missiles and prepared to fly air cover over Los Angeles and San Diego. We waited for word from Washington, D.C., regarding our next move. The Third Marine Aircraft Wing, headquartered at Miramar, received the instructions we were prepared for, which is to launch fighters to fly combat air patrols over Los Angeles. As the attacks unfolded in New York, Washington, D.C., and Pennsylvania, we were all shocked at what we were witnessing on television. However, unlike millions of Americans, we could not afford to be frozen to our seats. We had to be ready for action. Real action, and at the drop of a hat.

There were more questions than answers as we went into full combat mode. We all wondered who was behind such devastating attacks on our homeland. The obvious ran through our minds, and we discussed it a little. We thought maybe it was Islamic terrorists led by Osama Bin Laden. He had given us warnings years earlier. These are a patient people who wait for their moment of opportunity. In this case we later learned that they had plenty of time to practice as pilots, too, and here on American soil.

President Bush was in Florida during the attacks and was quickly flown to a secure location in Nebraska. From what I learned at the White House, I knew the President and Vice President would be safe from any follow-on attack. The

Presidential Emergency Operations Center (PEOC) under the White House was activated for Vice President Cheney and National Security Advisor, Condoleezza Rice, to perform their constitutional functions, while the President would run the country from his secret and secure Nebraska location.

At MCAS Miramar we strengthened security around the base perimeter and the flight line area. Rumors were flying that more terrorist aircraft were on their way to destroy more cities. I received a call that crop-dusting planes from the Imperial Valley were going to spray deadly chemicals on San Diego. Another caller said that Arab men were climbing the base perimeter fence trying to get on the base. A frantic lady reported that a white powdery substance was discovered near the day care center on base. All hell was breaking loose. We didn't know what to think from one minute to another, but we could only react to realities and wait for official instructions.

We received notice that the Federal Aviation Administration (FAA) closed down the skies over the United States to all airplanes and helicopters, both commercial and private. Inbound flights from overseas were diverted to Canada where they could land safely. United States military aircraft were the only aircraft allowed airborne. It was an eerie sight to see the vacant skies on the radar screen in the Operations Center. On a normal day there are thousands of aircraft in the air at any given moment.

After the 9/11 attacks, all U.S. military units went on their highest alert worldwide. We were still trying to understand what was going on and if there were any more planned attacks on the country. When information showed that the attacks were from the al-Qaeda terrorist group led by Osama Bin Laden, we began war plans to attack his training camps in Afghanistan.

President Bush made it clear that Bin Laden was wanted dead or alive, and within a few weeks after the attack, U.S. military forces were on the ground and in the air in Afghanistan attacking al-Qaeda and Taliban forces. Marines were sent to Afghanistan from Camp Pendleton, but the air war was conducted by Air Force aircraft. Our Marine air forces at MCAS Miramar continued to be on standby for any follow-on missions. The attack on Afghanistan was code named "Operation Enduring Freedom" and began on October 7, 2001. The stated goal of the invasion was to dismantle the al-Qaeda terrorist organization and end their use of Afghanistan as a base of their operations. The United States also said that it would remove the Taliban regime from power and create a viable Democratic state. This war would be the United States' longest running war in history. As history tells us, Bin Laden was finally located and killed by Navy Seals on May 2, 2011. The successful operation, code-named Operation Neptune Spear, was ordered by President Barack Obama. It took a long time, but we finally took down the man responsible for taking down our towers.

In July 2002 a good friend of mine, Brigadier General Harold "Baron" Fruchtnicht, was selected to take command of the 4th Marine Aircraft Wing, headquartered in New Orleans, Louisiana. He asked me to be his Chief of Staff and I eagerly accepted the three-year assignment that would mark the 30th year of my military career. Luci and I decided that I would go on this tour alone while she and the twins stayed in California. Luci had a steady job and the twins were in college, so there was no need to root them up for my final tour of duty.

The Brigadier General Selection Board was meeting in Washington, D. C., to select two new aviation generals from a pool of around 25 Colonels. I was being considered, but failed to be selected for the general ranks. I admit that I was a little disappointed, but I had made it to Colonel, and that was just fine. A good friend of mine was selected, Colonel Terry Robling, who is currently a three star general and doing a fantastic job for the Marine Corps. My rank of Colonel would carry me through to the end of my duty. Next stop: New Orleans.

I arrived in New Orleans in July 2002 and found a nice room in the French Quarter in the rear of a large mansion on Toulouse Street just a block from Bourbon Street. It was set in a quaint courtyard and was very secure, with large trees providing shade from the blistering sunrays. My place was also ideally located about three miles from my new office. The hustle and bustle of Bourbon Street, just a block away, was always a fun place to get a cold beer and to watch the crazy tourists make their way up and down the street. The French Quarter, also known as the Vieux Carré, is the oldest neighborhood in the city of New Orleans. Most of the French Quarter's buildings were built during the time of Spanish rule over New Orleans and this is reflected in its architecture. It is a combination of residential homes, hotels, guesthouses, bars, antique stores and tourist-oriented commercial properties.

As Chief of Staff of the 4th Marine Aircraft Wing (4th MAW) I oversaw the staff that worked for General Fruchtnicht, a Reserve General who lived in Houston and was present at the wing headquarters one weekend a month. In his absence from New Orleans I ensured the air wing functioned smoothly.

The Marine Corps has four air wings, three active and one reserve. Fourth MAW was the reserve wing, but the entire staff was on active duty. The air wing had flying units in California, Georgia, Pennsylvania, Maryland, Virginia, Arizona, Louisiana, Texas and New York. From New Orleans we controlled the operation of this diversified air wing to ensure that it was properly staffed, trained and funded.

Almost immediately after I arrived, two flying units were activated for combat duty to Afghanistan. Two helicopter squadrons were sent to the fight to engage the Taliban and al-Qaeda. Other units were being prepared for a possible invasion of Iraq to topple Saddam Hussein. My son, Mike, was sent to Kuwait with his squadron to prepare for the attack order on Iraq. He was flying with the F/A-18 squadron VMFA(AW)-225 Vikings. With my son now in the mix I kept up to speed on all the secret messages concerning an invasion date with a whole new perspective. Elements from all the Marine Air Wings were being sent to Kuwait.

On March 19, 2003 the invasion of Iraq began as American, British and Australian troops entered Iraq from Kuwait. President Bush and British Prime Minister Tony Blair stated that the coalition mission was "to disarm Iraq of weapons of mass destruction, to end Saddam Hussein's support for terrorism and to free the Iraqi people."

Massive air strikes across the country and against Iraqi command and control threw the defending army into chaos and prevented an effective resistance. The initial invasion collapsed the regime of Hussein in just 21 days. The invasion phase consisted of a conventionally fought war that concluded with the capture of the Iraq capital Baghdad. My son flew numerous combat missions during the invasion. Luci was now faced with the stress of Michael in combat after all she went through with my combat experiences. I tried to reassure her that things were going well with the war and Michael would be safe, but telling a mother not to worry is a lot like telling a grizzly bear not to eat fish. During the war, Michael, was awarded the same Air Medal my father and I earned. Three proud aviators!

At the 4th MAW headquarters we were working around the

clock to prepare and send aircraft units to the new fight in Iraq. Several more reserve units were activated and sent to Iraq to participate in combat operations. On May 1st an end of major combat operations was declared, ending the invasion period and beginning the military occupation period. What appeared to be a relatively smooth operation turned into a quagmire as Muslim factions began fighting and turned their anger on the liberating forces. More serious for the post-war state of Iraq was the looting of cached weaponry from military bases, which supplied the subsequent insurgency.

In April 2003, General Fruchtnicht was ordered by the Commanding General of Marine Forces Reserve, Lieutenant General Dennis McCarthy, to report to Central Command in Dubai, United Arabs Emirates, for duty. During his absence I took command of the 4th Marine Aircraft Wing, becoming the first Colonel to command the wing since 1960. This was a huge responsibility for me that I very much enjoyed. I loved being in command of Marines, and this challenge gave me one last hurrah before I would be forced to retire in 2004. Even though I never made the rank of Brigadier General, I did what many Marine Corps Aviator Generals never did, command an air wing. Be it only a couple of months, I was once again "king." On weekends I found the time to visit the various units and fly in their aircraft throughout the air wing. General Fruchtnicht returned to his duties after returning from the combat zone, and I reverted back to my duties as his Chief of Staff.

In the summer of 2004 a good friend of mine who is a Captain with Jet Blue Airways called me to see if I would be interested in a flying job with the airlines when I retired. I was looking for some kind of follow-on job that would keep me flying and this fit perfectly into my plans. I interviewed with airline officials and was offered an immediate position with the airline. I was torn. Though I looked forward to a job as a commercial pilot, I knew I would miss my days in the military. The two just don't compare.

On July 20, 2004, I strapped into an F/A-18 with the "Gators" of VMFA-142 in Atlanta and took off for my final military flight. I didn't want the flight to end, but after about an hour in the air I lowered the gear and landed the Hornet for the final time. I then packed up my belongings and headed out of New Orleans. I watched it disappear in the rear view mirror as I got on the road back to California and my family.

On October 1, 2004 at a ceremony at MCAS Miramar in San Diego I was officially retired from the Marine Corps. My family, father and friends were all there to celebrate the end of my long Marine Corps career. When it came time during the ceremony to review the troops, I took my father and together we walked in front of the platoons of troops and bid farewell. It was a scene to remember for us both.

I had asked my dad to again wear his military uniform and he was proud as a peacock that day. I talked briefly to the audience, thanking everyone that had a role in my career, especially Luci and my children. To conclude the ceremony Gunnery Sergeant Lisa Leighton read a letter from President Bush and the Commandant of the Marine Corps thanking me for my many years of service. Then the band played the Marines Hymn, and standing at attention and listening to the music my eyes welled up. I couldn't help myself. I'm a big man physically, but this fanfare was melting me just a little. In my heart I felt a tremendous pride for my country. I was proud to have served, and I'd do it again given the chance.

CHAPTER 42

I immediately went into training in Miami for Jet Blue to fly as a First Officer of the A320 Airbus. After initially being based in New York for a few months I transferred to Long Beach, California, which was only about 30 miles from my home. Twice a week I flew from Long Beach to New York, Boston or Washington, D.C. Now, I won't say that I didn't enjoy flying the big planes, but it just wasn't the same thrill of flying fighters, so after three years with the airline I left to spend more time at home and with my wife. I bought a new Yamaha Raider S motorcycle to ride the roads of southern California and beyond. I also purchased a golden retriever and named him Reagan, after our 40th President. He still keeps us company every day.

Kristen and Kathy graduated from San Diego State University in 2005, and received their teaching credentials and Masters Degrees at California State University, Fullerton. They both were immediately hired with the Irvine Unified School District as elementary school teachers. Kathy teaches 6th grade and Kristen teaches 5th grade. They both love what they do for a living. Kristen got married in July 2010 and has a baby girl, and Kathy got married in Dec 2012. Michael left active duty from the Marine Corps in 2007 and went to work for a Fortune

500 company in Austin, Texas, where he reports being very happy.

On the sixth anniversary of 9/11, my mother passed away. She left this world to rejoin her mother whom she lost in 1933, and her sister Rita. My mother's passing was a sad event, but it had been difficult and even sadder to see her deteriorate mentally from the cruel effects of Alzheimer's. When she died, my siblings and I felt that she could now be at peace. At the time of this writing, my father is 95 years old and is confined to a wheelchair, but is doing well. He lives in an assisted living home in Glendale, Arizona where he has several friends and often talks about his days in the military. My brother Steve, who recently retired, visits dad frequently to ensure he is doing well. My other siblings in the Phoenix area also go by to see dad to provide assistance.

I received a call in September 2009 from Bourgade High School notifying me that I was to be inducted in the Hall of Fame. The Bourgade Catholic High School Hall of Fame is dedicated to those outstanding individuals who, through their accomplishments, have brought honor to themselves and the Bourgade Catholic Community. This was a complete surprise to me and I was humbled. Luci and I went to the induction ceremony in November, and along with four other alumni, I received a nice engraved glass trophy at the banquet. With this induction I felt nostalgia for my old classmates, so I made the effort to get my high school class together for our 40th class reunion in 2011.

On October 1, 2011, about 65% of our class got together in Phoenix for our 40th class reunion. Where did the time go? We had the reunion at the Arrowhead Country Club. Our classmate Tom McCarthy and his brothers Dave and Matt play in a classic rock band, so they provided the entertainment. My high school girlfriend Kathy was there with her husband Thurman, and we reminisced and laughed about the days of old. Nick and Lori, married for 37 years, looked as good together as ever. Other high school sweethearts that married soon after high school – Ken Groom and Melissa Adams, and Chet Garry and Ruth Vukovich – said their marriages were going strong and I learned they had children and grandchildren. The latter always shocks me. Are we really THAT age where we can have grandchildren? I guess so.

I invited Jimmy O'Connor's children to attend the function to represent their father. Only one daughter could join us. O'Connor's baby girl, Julie, now age 30, attended and grew very emotional as she listened to stories about her father that she never heard before. Since the reunion I reconnected with Erin and Paul, Jim's other two children.

My football coach, Bill Maas, made the reunion with his wife. Several of the team members were there, too, carrying a few extra pounds, some grey hair… or little hair at all. We took pictures, laughed and danced. No one wanted to call it a night. We didn't want the party to end, so we simply moved outside and continued with our stories. It was like we never left high school. No one talked much about the 40 years that passed because we put ourselves back on the small campus and tried to relive those "happy days" of the late '60s and early '70s, days I will never, ever forget.

Now what is in the future for Greg Raths? As I send this to printing in the spring of 2013, I just completed my Bachelor of Arts degree at California State University, Fullerton in History and Political Science. I have also just formed an exploratory committee to test the waters for a run for Congress for the U.S. House of Representative for California's 45th Congressional District. I put together a plan, and I am now executing it; with hard work and some "luck" I will be Congressman Gregory G. Raths (R-CA) in January 2015.

With President Bill Clinton in The Oval Office,
Washington, D.C. 1998.

Christmas party at the White House. Dancing with
Luci in the East Room, Christmas, 1997.

At the White House Staff Dining Room with
my parents, 1998.

Christmas picture with the President and First Lady, 1998.

Christmas at the White House, 1998.

In the Red Room at the White House, 1998.

At Camp David with Luci and the twins, 1998.

Promotion Ceremony to Colonel in the East Wing Reception
Room. The Honorable Alan Sullivan and Luci pinning
on my Eagles, January 1998.

Boarding Air Force One at Andrews Air Force Base,
Maryland, 1999.

Saying farewell to President Clinton. Oval Yellow Room, 1999.

My final flight on Air Force One in the Aircraft's Conference
Room with Secretary of Transportation Rodney Slater,
Doug Sosnick, and Kirk Hamlin, 1999.

Taking command of Marine Aircraft Group 46, MCAS
Miramar, San Diego, California, June 6, 1999, with my father.

Me and my son, First Lieutenant Michael Raths, USMC, 2000.

Addressing my Marine Corps troops, MCAS Miramar,
California, 2000.

My superb Adjutant Staff of MAG-46, Gunnery Sergeant
Cynthia Manderfield, Captain Adzekai Kuma, and
Staff Sergeant Lisa Leighton, 2000.

MAG-46 Group Commander in my F/A-18A Hornet, MCAS
Miramar, California, 1999-2001.

My son, Mike, flying with me in an F/A-18D Hornet,
MCAS Miramar, California, 2000.

On a stop-over flight at Sky Harbor International Airport,
Phoenix, Arizona. Mr. Tom McCarthy, me, brothers Bob
and Dan, and good friend, Dan O'Connor, 2001.

My Retirement Ceremony at MCAS Miramar, San Diego, California. With Luci, Kristen and Kathryn, October 1, 2004.

With my father and brother Bob at my Retirement Ceremony.

Retirement shadow box gift from fellow officers, 2004.

Aboard my 2006 Yamaha Raider motorcycle, 2006.

At the Laughlin Nevada Motorcycle River Run, 2007.

Jet Blue First Officer of the Airbus 320, 2007.

My dog Reagan, 2008.

My good friend, Bruce "Lash Larue" Paul at a
VMFP-3 Squadron Reunion, Quantico, Virginia, 2011.

Memorial Golf Tournament for Jimmy O'Connor and his
father and uncles in Phoenix, Arizona, with my good friends,
Danny Fontana and Nick Ganem, 2012.

Bourgade High School 40th Class reunion, October, 2011 in
Glendale, Arizona. Back row: Chet Garry, Tom Reilly,
Mike Kelly; Next row: Coach Bill Maas and Nick Ganem;
Next Row, me, Julie O'Connor (Jim's daughter),
Dave Sanchez and Ed VanDerWerf; sitting, Mike LePert.

With the Commandant of the Marine Corps,
General James F. Amos, USMC, at an F-4 Phantom II
Reunion, San Diego, November 2012.

In remembrance to my aviator friends who have passed

Colonel Jim French

Colonel Denny Fitz

Lieutenant Colonel Larry Reiman

Lieutenant Colonel Bert Sperry

Lieutenant Colonel Ray Priest

Major Cheyenne Bowdie

Major Jaws Kittle

Major John Spaar

Major Slim Fullerton

Major Spock Neal

Captain Dick Hubbard

Captain Michael Novotny

Captain Lee Barthel

Captain Pete Keenan

Captain Bill Lauerman

First Lieutenant Pete Rabczewski

ACRONYMS

A-6E	Marine Corps and Navy heavy attack jet aircraft
A-7	Navy light-attack jet aircraft
A-20	World War II vintage twin engine attack aircraft
AF-1	Air Force One, Presidential Aircraft
AH-1W	Marine Corps attack helicopter
AFB	Air Force Base
ASU	Arizona State University
BHS	Bourgade High School
Blue Angels	Navy Flight Demonstration Team
CH-46E	Marine Corps Medium lift helicopter
CH-53E	Marine Corps Heavy lift helicopter
CAG	Navy Carrier Air Group Commander
Call Sign	Nickname military pilots are given by squadron mates
COC	Combat Operations Center

CAT	Crisis Action Team of highly trained Secret Service agents
CNN	Cable News Network
CNO	Chief of Naval Operations
CAW	Navy Carrier Air Wing consisting of about 8 squadrons and detachments
CO	Commanding Officer, Commander of a military unit
CV	Conventional powered aircraft carrier
CVBG	Aircraft Carrier Battle Group
CVN	Nuclear powered aircraft carrier
CVW	Carrier Air Wing
D-Day	June 6, 1944, World War II Allied invasion of Normandy, France
DOD	Department of Defense
EA-6B	Marine Corps and Navy Electronic Warfare Aircraft
FAA	Federal Aviation Administration
F/A-18A/C	Marine Corps and Navy single seat fighter attack jet aircraft

F/A-18D	Marine Corps two seat all-weather fighter attack jet aircraft
F-4	Military fighter jet aircraft used by USMC, USN, and USAF
F-14	Navy fighter jet aircraft
FCLP	Field Carrier Landing Practice
FMF	Fleet Marine Force
G Force	Force of gravity on the body as an aircraft accelerated or turns rapidly
HARM	High Speed Anti-Radiation Missile
HMH	Marine Corps heavy lift helicopter squadron
HMLA	Marine Corps light attack helicopter squadron
HMM	Marine Corps medium lift helicopter squadron
HMX-1	Presidential Helicopter Squadron based at Quantico, Virginia
JFC	Joint Forces Command
KC-130	Marine Corps tanker aircraft
KC-135	Air Force tanker aircraft
LSO	Landing Signal Officer

M-14	Marine Corps rifle
M-16	Marine Corps Automatic Assault Rifle
MAG	Marine Corps Aircraft Group comprising of about eight squadrons
MALS	Marine Corps Aviation Logistics Squadron
MASS	Marine Air Support Squadron
MAW	Marine Corps Air Wing comprising of about four air groups
MAWTS	Marine Aircraft Weapons and Tactics Squadron
MCAS	Marine Corps Air Station
MEF	Marine Corps Expeditionary Force
NAS	Naval Air Station
NASCAR	National Association for Stock Car Auto Racing
NATO	North Atlantic Treaty Organization
NBC	National Broadcasting Company
NOLA	New Orleans, Louisiana
OSO	Officer Selection Officer
PIO	Pilot induced oscillations of an aircraft, small movements up and down

PEOC	Presidential Emergency Operations Center underneath the White House
PCC	Phoenix Community College
POTUS	President of the United States
RF-4B	Marine Corps tactical reconnaissance aircraft
ROK	Republic of Korea
ROTC	Reserve Officer Training Course
Squadron	Military flying unit consisting of about 12 aircraft and 200 personnel
STP	Fuel and oil additives for automobiles
TACAN	Tactical Air Navigation system used by military aircraft
T2-C	Navy twin jet engine trainer
T-34B	Navy single prop engine trainer
T/A-4	Navy single engine jet trainer
UH-1N	Marine Corps utility helicopter
UPI	United Press International
USA	United States Army
USAF	United States Air Force

USCG	United States Coast Guard
USMC	United States Marine Corps
USN	United States Navy
USS	United States military ship
VMFA	Marine Fighter Attack Squadron
VMFA(AW)	All-Weather Marine Fighter Attack Squadron
VMFP	Marine Tactical Reconnaissance Squadron
VMFT	Marine Fighter Training Squadron
VPOTUS	Vice President of the United States
VT	Navy Training Squadron
WHCA	White House Communication Agency
WHMO	White House Military Office
WMD	Weapon of Mass Destruction
WTI	Weapons and Tactics Instructor
XO	Executive Officer, Number two in charge of a military unit
Y2K	The Millennium computer virus or bug